Kewaunee County, Wisconsin

Martha Martin

Contents

Overview of Kewaunee County — 1
- Kewaunee County, Wisconsin — 1
- Wisconsin — 6

History — 31
- Ojibwe language — 31
- Potawatomi language — 50

Geography — 56
- West Alaska Lake — 56
- Kettle Moraine — 57
- Krohns Lake — 58
- Green Bay (Lake Michigan) — 59
- East Alaska Lake — 60

Cities and Towns in Kewaunee County — 61
- Ahnapee, Wisconsin — 61
- Carlton, Wisconsin — 64
- Casco, Wisconsin — 66
- Franklin, Kewaunee County, Wisconsin — 69
- Kewaunee, Wisconsin — 71
- Lincoln, Kewaunee County, Wisconsin — 74
- Luxemburg, Wisconsin — 77
- Pierce, Wisconsin — 81

Counties Nearby to Visit — 83
- Door County, Wisconsin — 83
- Manitowoc County, Wisconsin — 91

| Brown County, Wisconsin | 97 |

Things to See In and Around Kewaunee County — **103**

Algoma Pierhead Light	103
Gravel Island National Wildlife Refuge	105
Kewaunee Pierhead Light	108
Green Bay National Wildlife Refuge	110
Holland Harbor Light	114

Transportation — **118**

Wisconsin Highway 29	118
Wisconsin Highway 42	126
Wisconsin Highway 54	130
Wisconsin Highway 57	132

References

| Article Sources and Contributors | 137 |
| Image Sources, Licenses and Contributors | 138 |

Overview of Kewaunee County

Kewaunee County, Wisconsin

Kewaunee County, Wisconsin	
 Location in the state of Wisconsin	
 Wisconsin's location in the U.S.	
Founded	*information needed*
Seat	Kewaunee
Largest city	Algoma
Area - Total - Land - Water	1085 sq mi (2809 km²) 343 sq mi (887 km²) 742 sq mi (1921 km²), 68.41%
Population - **(2000)** - Density	20187 59/sq mi (23/km²)
Time zone	Central: UTC-6/-5
Website	www.kewauneeco.org [1]

Kewaunee County is a county located in the U.S. state of Wisconsin. As of 2000, the population was 20,187. Its county seat is Kewaunee. Kewaunee County is part of the Green Bay Metropolitan Statistical Area.

Geography

According to the U.S. Census Bureau, the county has a total area of 1,085 square miles (2,809 km²), of which 343 square miles (887 km²) is land and 742 square miles (1,921 km²) (68.41%) is water.

Adjacent counties

- Door County - north
- Manitowoc County - south
- Brown County - west

Major highways

- 29 Highway 29 (Wisconsin)
- 42 Highway 42 (Wisconsin)
- 54 Highway 54 (Wisconsin)
- 57 Highway 57 (Wisconsin)

Demographics

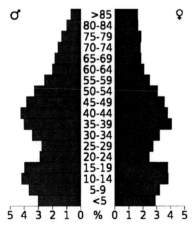

2000 Census Age Pyramid for Kewaunee County.

Historical populations			
Census	Pop.		%±
1900	17212		—
1910	16784		−2.5%
1920	16091		−4.1%
1930	16037		−0.3%
1940	16680		4.0%
1950	17366		4.1%
1960	18282		5.3%
1970	18961		3.7%
1980	19539		3.0%
1990	18878		−3.4%
2000	20187		6.9%
WI Counties 1900-1990 [2]			

As of the census of 2000, there were 20,187 people, 7,623 households, and 5,549 families residing in the county. The population density was 59 people per square mile (23/km²). There were 8,221 housing units at an average density of 24 per square mile (9/km²). The racial makeup of the county was 98.56% White, 0.15% Black or African American, 0.27% Native American, 0.13% Asian, 0.30% from other races, and 0.57% from two or more races. 0.76% of the population were Hispanic or Latino of any race. 36.4% were of German, 23.8% Belgian, 9.7% Czech, 6.3% Polish and 5.1% American ancestry according to Census 2000.

There were 7,623 households out of which 33.50% had children under the age of 18 living with them, 62.40% were married couples living together, 6.60% had a female householder with no husband present, and 27.20% were non-families. 23.50% of all households were made up of individuals and 11.80% had someone living alone who was 65 years of age or older. The average household size was 2.61 and the average family size was 3.10.

In the county, the population was spread out with 25.80% under the age of 18, 8.00% from 18 to 24, 28.20% from 25 to 44, 22.80% from 45 to 64, and 15.20% who were 65 years of age or older. The median age was 38 years. For every 100 females there were 100.60 males. For every 100 females age 18 and over, there were 98.80 males.

Cities, villages, and towns

- Ahnapee
- Algoma
- Carlton
- Casco (town)
- Casco
- Franklin
- Kewaunee
- Lincoln
- Luxemburg (town)
- Luxemburg
- Montpelier
- Pierce
- Red River
- West Kewaunee

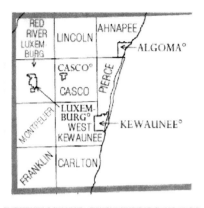

Unincorporated communities

- Alaska
- Casco Junction
- Dyckesville (partial)

Welcome sign on WIS 54, farm in the background

- East Krok
- Krok
- Pilsen
- Rankin
- Rio Creek
- Rosiere (partial)
- Ryans Corner
- Tonet
- Walhain

Images

Kewaunee County Courthouse

Kewaunee County fairgrounds

External links
- Kewaunee County [3]
- Northeast Wisconsin Historical County Plat Maps & Atlases [4] University of Wisconsin Digital Collections Center

Geographical coordinates: 44°35′N 87°26′W

Wisconsin

State of Wisconsin	
Flag	Seal
Nickname(s): Badger State; America's Dairyland	
Motto(s): Forward	
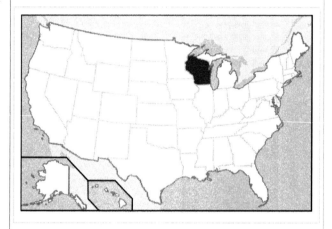	
Official language(s)	**De jure**: None **De facto**: English
Demonym	Wisconsinite
Capital	Madison
Largest city	Milwaukee
Largest metro area	Milwaukee metropolitan area
Area	Ranked 23rd in the US
- Total	65,498 sq mi (169,639 km^2)
- Width	260 miles (420 km)
- Length	310 miles (500 km)

- % water	17
- Latitude	42° 30′ N to 47° 05′ N
- Longitude	86° 46′ W to 92° 53′ W
Population	Ranked 20th in the US
- Total	5,654,774
- Density	98.8/sq mi (38.13/km^2) Ranked 23rd in the US
- Median income	$47,220 (15th)
Elevation	
- Highest point	Timms Hill 1,951 ft (595 m)
- Mean	1,050 ft (320 m)
- Lowest point	Lake Michigan 579 ft (176 m)
Admission to Union	May 29, 1848 (30th)
Governor	Jim Doyle (D)
Lieutenant Governor	Barbara Lawton (D)
Legislature	Wisconsin Legislature
- Upper house	Senate
- Lower house	State Assembly
U.S. Senators	Herb Kohl (D) Russ Feingold (D)
U.S. House delegation	List
Time zone	Central: UTC-6/-5
Abbreviations	WI Wis. US-WI
Website	http://www.wisconsin.gov

Wisconsin ([i] /wɪˈskɑnsɪn/) is a U.S. state located in the north-central United States and is considered part of the Midwest. It is bordered by Minnesota to the west, Iowa to the southwest, Illinois to the south, Lake Michigan to the east, Upper Michigan to the northeast, and Lake Superior to the north. Wisconsin's capital is Madison, and its largest city is Milwaukee. As of 2009 the state has an estimated 5.6 million residents. The state contains 72 counties.

Etymology

The word *Wisconsin* has its origins in the name given to the Wisconsin River by one of the Algonquian speaking American Indian groups living in the region at the time of European contact. French explorer Jacques Marquette was the first European to reach the Wisconsin River and record its name, arriving in 1673 and calling the river *Meskousing* in his journal. This spelling was later corrupted to *Ouisconsin* by other French explorers, and over time this version became the French name for both the Wisconsin River and the surrounding lands. English speakers anglicized the spelling to its modern form when they began to arrive in greater numbers during the early 19th Century. The current spelling was made official by the legislature of Wisconsin Territory in 1845.

Through the course of its many variations, the Algonquian source word for Wisconsin and its original meaning have both grown obscure. Interpretations may vary, but most implicate the river and the red sandstone that line its banks. One leading theory holds that the name originated from the Miami word *Meskonsing*, meaning "it lies red," a reference to the setting of the Wisconsin River as it flows by the reddish sandstone of the Wisconsin Dells. Numerous other theories have also been widely publicized, including claims that name originated from one of a variety of Ojibwa words meaning "red stone place," "gathering of the waters," or "great rock."

History

Main article: History of Wisconsin

Wisconsin has been home to a wide variety of cultures over the past twelve thousand years. The first people arrived around 10000 BCE during the Wisconsin Glaciation. These early inhabitants, called Paleo-Indians, hunted now-extinct ice age animals exemplified by the Boaz mastodon, a prehistoric mastodon skeleton unearthed along with spear points in southwest Wisconsin. After the ice age ended around 8000 BCE, people in the subsequent Archaic period lived by hunting, fishing, and gathering food from wild plants. Agricultural societies emerged gradually over the Woodland period between 1000 BCE to 1000 CE. Towards the end of this period, Wisconsin was the heartland of the "Effigy Mound culture," which built thousands of animal-shaped mounds across the landscape. Later, between 1000 and 1500 CE, the Mississippian and Oneota cultures

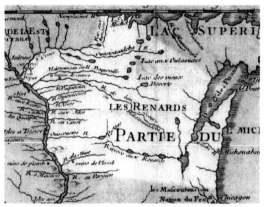

Wisconsin in 1718, Guillaume de L'Isle map, approximate state area highlighted.

built substantial settlements including the fortified village at Aztalan in southeast Wisconsin. The Oneota may be the ancestors of the modern Ioway and Ho-Chunk tribes, who shared the Wisconsin region with the Menominee at the time of European contact. Other American Indian groups living in Wisconsin when Europeans first settled included the Ojibwa, Sauk, Fox, Kickapoo, and Pottawatomie, who migrated to Wisconsin from the east between 1500 and 1700.

Jean Nicolet, depicted in this recent painting, was probably the first European to explore Wisconsin.

The first European to visit what became Wisconsin was probably the French explorer Jean Nicolet. He canoed west from Georgian Bay through the Great Lakes in 1634, and it is traditionally assumed that he came ashore near Green Bay at Red Banks. Pierre Radisson and Médard des Groseilliers visited Green Bay again in 1654–1666 and Chequamegon Bay in 1659–1660, where they traded for fur with local American Indians. In 1673, Jacques Marquette and Louis Jolliet became the first to record a journey on the Fox-Wisconsin Waterway all the way to the Mississippi River near Prairie du Chien. Frenchmen like Nicholas Perrot continued to ply the fur trade across Wisconsin through the 17th and 18th centuries, but the French made no permanent settlements in Wisconsin before Great Britain won control of the region following the French and Indian War in 1763. Even so, French traders continued to work in the region after the war, and some, beginning with Charles de Langlade in 1764, now settled in Wisconsin permanently rather than returning to British-controlled Canada.

Wisconsin became a territorial possession of the United States in 1783 after the American Revolutionary War. However, the British remained in de facto control until after the War of 1812, which finally established an American presence in the area. Under American control, the economy of the territory shifted from fur trading to lead mining. The prospect of easy mineral wealth drew immigrants from throughout the U.S. and Europe to the lead deposits located at Mineral Point, Wisconsin and nearby areas. Some miners found shelter in the holes they had dug and earned the nickname "badgers," leading to Wisconsin's identity as the "Badger State." The sudden influx of white miners prompted tension with the local Native American population. The Winnebago War of 1827 and the Black Hawk War of 1832 led to the forced removal of American Indians from most parts of the state. Following these conflicts, Wisconsin Territory was organized in 1836. Continued white settlement led to statehood in 1848.

The Little White Schoolhouse in Ripon, Wisconsin held the nation's first meeting of the Republican Party

Politics in early Wisconsin were defined by the greater national debate over slavery. A free state from its foundation, Wisconsin became a center of northern abolitionism. The debate became especially intense in 1854 after a runaway slave from Missouri named Joshua Glover was captured in Racine. Glover was taken into custody under the Federal Fugitive Slave Law, but a mob of abolitionists stormed the prison where Glover was held and helped him escape to Canada. The Wisconsin Supreme Court ultimately declared the Fugitive Slave Law unconstitutional in a trial stemming from the incident. The Republican Party, founded on March 20, 1854 by anti-slavery expansion activists in Ripon, Wisconsin, grew to dominate state politics in the aftermath of these events. During the Civil War, around 91,000 troops from Wisconsin fought for the Union.

Wisconsin's economy also diversified during the early years of statehood. While lead mining diminished, agriculture became a principal occupation in the southern half of the state. Railroads were built across the state to help transport grains to

Drawing of Industrial Milwaukee in 1882

market, and industries like J.I. Case & Company in Racine were founded to build agricultural equipment. Wisconsin briefly became one of the nation's leading producers of wheat during the 1860s. Meanwhile, the lumber industry dominated in the heavily forested northern sections of Wisconsin, and sawmills sprung up in cities like La Crosse, Eau Claire, and Wausau. These economic activities had dire environmental consequences. By the close of the 19th century, intensive agriculture had devastated soil fertility, and lumbering had deforested most of the state. This forced both wheat agriculture and the lumber industry into a precipitous decline.

The Daniel E. Krause Stone Barn in Chase, Wisconsin was built in 1903 as dairy farming spread across the state

Beginning in the 1890s, farmers in Wisconsin shifted from wheat to dairy production in order to make more sustainable and profitable use of their land. Many immigrants carried cheese making traditions that, combined with the state's suitable geography and dairy research led by Stephen Babcock at the University of Wisconsin, helped the state build a reputation as "America's Dairyland." Meanwhile, conservationists including Aldo Leopold helped reestablish the state's forests during the early 20th century. This paved the way for a more renewable lumber and paper milling industry as well as promoting recreational tourism in the northern woodlands. Manufacturing also boomed in Wisconsin during the early 20th century, driven by an immense immigrant workforce arriving from Europe. Industries in cities like Milwaukee ranged from brewing and food processing to heavy machine production and toolmaking, leading Wisconsin to rank 8th among U.S. states in total product value by 1910.

The early 20th century was also notable for the emergence of progressive politics championed by Robert M. La Follette. Between 1901 and 1914, Progressive Republicans in Wisconsin created the nation's first comprehensive statewide primary election system, the first effective workplace injury compensation law, and the first state income tax, making taxation proportional to actual earnings. The progressive Wisconsin Idea also promoted the statewide expansion of the University of Wisconsin through the UW-Extension system at this time. Later, UW economics professors John R. Commons and Harold Groves helped Wisconsin create the first unemployment compensation program in the United States in 1932.

Wisconsin Governor Robert La Follette addressing an assembly in Decatur, Illinois, 1905.

Wisconsin took part in several political extremes in the mid to late 20th century, ranging from the anti-communist hysteria of Senator Joseph McCarthy in the 1950s to the radical antiwar protests at UW-Madison that culminated in the Sterling Hall bombing in August 1970. Recent politics have been comparatively moderate, but the state has continued to push forward new ideas, most notably becoming a leader in welfare reform under Republican Governor Tommy Thompson during the 1990s. The state's economy also underwent further transformations towards the close of the century, as heavy industry and manufacturing declined in favor of a service economy based on medicine, education, agribusiness, and tourism.

The U.S. Navy battleship, USS *Wisconsin*, was named in honor of this state.

Geography

Wisconsin is bordered by the Montreal River; Lake Superior and Michigan to the north; by Lake Michigan to the east; by Illinois to the south; and by Iowa to the southwest and Minnesota to the northwest. A border dispute with Michigan was settled by two cases, both Wisconsin v. Michigan, in 1934 and 1935. The state's boundaries include the Mississippi River and St. Croix River in the west, and the Menominee River in the northeast. Wisconsin is the northernmost state that does not share a border with Canada.

With its location between the Great Lakes and the Mississippi River, Wisconsin is home to a wide variety of geographical features. The state is divided into five distinct regions. In the north, the Lake Superior Lowland occupies a belt of land along Lake Superior. Just to the south, the Northern Highland has massive mixed hardwood and coniferous forests including the 1500000 acres (6100 km^2) Chequamegon-Nicolet National Forest, as well as thousands of glacial lakes, and the state's highest point, Timms Hill. In the middle of the state, the Central Plain has some unique sandstone formations like the Dells of the Wisconsin River in addition to rich farmland.

Wisconsin can be divided into five geographic regions.

The Eastern Ridges and Lowlands region in the southeast is home to many of Wisconsin's largest cities. The ridges include the Niagara Escarpment, that stretches from New York State, the Black River Escarpment and the Magnesian Escarpment. The bedrock of the Niagara Escarpment is dolomite, while the two shorter ridges have limestone bedrock. In the southwest, the Western Upland is a rugged landscape with a mix of forest and farmland, including many bluffs on the Mississippi River. This region is part of the Driftless Area, which also includes portions of Iowa, Illinois, and Minnesota. This area was not covered by glaciers during the most recent ice age, the Wisconsin Glaciation.

The Driftless Area of southwestern Wisconsin is characterized by bluffs carved in sedimentary rock by water from melting Ice Age glaciers.

Overall, 46% of Wisconsin's land area is covered by forest. Langlade County has a soil rarely found outside of the county called Antigo Silt Loam.

Areas under the management of the National Park Service include the following:

- Apostle Islands National Lakeshore along Lake Superior
- Ice Age National Scenic Trail
- North Country National Scenic Trail
- Saint Croix National Scenic Riverway

There is one national forest managed by the U.S. Forest Service in Wisconsin, Chequamegon-Nicolet National Forest.

Wisconsin has sister-state relationships with the Germany's Hesse, Japan's Chiba Prefecture, Mexico's Jalisco, China's Heilongjiang, and Nicaragua.

Climate

Wisconsin's climate is classified as humid continental. The highest temperature ever recorded in the state was in the Wisconsin Dells, on July 13, 1936, where it reached 114 °F (46 °C). The lowest temperature ever recorded in Wisconsin was in the village of Couderay, where it reached −55 °F (−48 °C) on both February 2 and February 4, 1996.

Monthly Normal High and Low Temperatures For Selected Wisconsin Cities [°F (°C)]												
City	Jan	Feb	Mar	Apr	May	Jun	Jul	Aug	Sep	Oct	Nov	Dec
Green Bay	24/7 (−4/-14)	29/12 (−2/-11)	40/23 (4/-5)	55/34 (13/1)	68/45 (20/7)	77/54 (25/12)	81/59 (27/15)	78/56 (26/13)	70/48 (21/9)	58/37 (14/3)	42/26 (6/-3)	29/13 (−2/-11)
La Crosse	26/6 (−3/-14)	32/13 (0/-11)	45/24 (7/-4)	60/37 (16/3)	72/49 (22/9)	81/58 (27/14)	85/63 (29/17)	82/61 (28/16)	74/52 (23/11)	61/40 (16/4)	44/27 (7/-3)	30/14 (−1/-10)
Madison	25/9 (−4/-13)	31/14 (−1/-10)	43/25 (6/-4)	57/35 (14/2)	69/46 (21/8)	78/56 (26/13)	82/61 (28/16)	79/59 (26/15)	71/50 (22/10)	60/39 (16/4)	43/28 (6/-2)	30/16 (−1/-9)
Milwaukee	28/13 (−2/-11)	32/18 (0/-8)	43/27 (6/-3)	54/36 (12/2)	66/46 (19/8)	76/56 (24/13)	81/63 (27/17)	79/62 (26/17)	72/54 (22/12)	60/43 (16/6)	46/31 (8/-1)	33/19 (1/-7)
[1]												

Demographics

Historical populations		
Census	Pop.	%±
1820	1444	—
1830	3635	151.7%
1840	30945	751.3%
1850	305391	886.9%
1860	775881	154.1%
1870	1054670	35.9%
1880	1315457	24.7%
1890	1693330	28.7%
1900	2069042	22.2%
1910	2333860	12.8%
1920	2632067	12.8%
1930	2939006	11.7%
1940	3137587	6.8%
1950	3434575	9.5%
1960	3951777	15.1%

1970	4417731	11.8%
1980	4705767	6.5%
1990	4891769	4.0%
2000	5363675	9.6%
Est. 2009	5654774	5.4%

According to the U.S. Census Bureau, as of 2000, Wisconsin had a population of 5,363,675. Wisconsin's population was reported as 6.4% under the age of 5, 25.5% under 18, and 13.1% were 65 or older. Females made up approximately 50.6% of the population.

Since its founding, Wisconsin has been ethnically heterogeneous. Following the period of French fur traders, the next wave of settlers were miners, many of whom were Cornish, who settled the southwestern area of the state. The next wave was dominated by "Yankees," migrants from New England and upstate New York; in the early years of statehood, they dominated the state's heavy industry, finance, politics and education. Between 1850 and 1900, large numbers of European immigrants followed them, including Germans, Scandinavians (the largest group being Norwegian), and smaller groups of Belgians, Dutch, Swiss, Finns, Irish, Poles, Portuguese and others. In the 20th century, large numbers of Mexicans and African Americans came, settling mainly in Milwaukee; and after end of the Vietnam War came a new influx of Hmongs.

The five largest ancestry groups in Wisconsin are: German (42.6%), Irish (10.9%), Polish (9.3%), Norwegian (8.5%), English (6.5%). German is the most common ancestry in every county in the state, except Menominee, Trempealeau and Vernon. Wisconsin has the highest percentage of residents of Polish ancestry of any state. The various ethnic groups settled in different areas of the state. Although Germans settled throughout the state, the largest concentration was in Milwaukee. Norwegians settled in lumbering and farming areas in the north and west. Small colonies of Belgians, Swiss, Finns and other groups settled in their particular areas, with Irish, Italian, and Polish immigrants settling primarily in urban areas. African Americans came to Milwaukee, especially from 1940 on. Menominee County is the only county in the eastern United States with an American Indian majority.

					Demographics of Wisconsin (csv) [2]
By race	**White**	**Black**	**AIAN***	**Asian**	**NHPI***
2000 (total population)	91.52%	6.15%	1.30%	1.92%	0.08%
2000 (Hispanic only)	3.35%	0.17%	0.11%	0.03%	0.01%
2005 (total population)	91.00%	6.48%	1.30%	2.21%	0.09%
2005 (Hispanic only)	4.17%	0.20%	0.12%	0.04%	0.01%
Growth 2000–05 (total population)	2.64%	8.89%	3.13%	18.59%	6.85%

Growth 2000–05 (non-Hispanic only)	1.65%	8.53%	2.43%	18.63%	6.18%
Growth 2000–05 (Hispanic only)	28.67%	21.23%	10.54%	16.75%	10.87%
* AIAN is American Indian or Alaskan Native; NHPI is Native Hawaiian or Pacific Islander					

86% of Wisconsin's African-American population live in four cities: Milwaukee, Racine, Beloit, Kenosha, with Milwaukee home to nearly three-fourths of the state's black Americans. Milwaukee is among the 10 major U.S. cities with the most African Americans per capita.[*citation needed*] In the Great Lakes region, only Detroit and Cleveland have a higher percentage of African-American residents.

33% of Wisconsin's Asian population is Hmong, with significant communities in Milwaukee, Wausau, Green Bay, Sheboygan, Appleton, Madison, La Crosse, Eau Claire, Oshkosh, and Manitowoc.

Religion

Christianity is the predominant religion of Wisconsin. As of the year 2000, the RCMS reported that the three largest denominational groups in Wisconsin are Catholic, Mainline Protestant, and Evangelical Protestant. The Catholic Church has the highest number of adherents in Wisconsin (at 1,695,660), followed by the Evangelical Lutheran Church in America with 463,432 members reported and the Lutheran Church--Missouri Synod, reporting 241,306 adherents. The percentage of Wisconsin residents who belong to various affiliations are shown below:

The Roman Catholic Shrine of Our Lady of Guadalupe, in La Crosse, Wisconsin

- Christian – 80%
  - Protestant – 50%
    - Lutheran – 23%
    - Methodist – 7%
    - Baptist – 5%
    - Presbyterian – 2%
    - United Church of Christ – 2%
    - Other Protestant or general Protestant – 15%
  - Roman Catholic – 29%
  - Other Christian – 1%

- Other religions – 1%
- Non-affiliated – 15%

Law and government

The capital is Madison, Wisconsin.

State Executive Officers

- Governor: James Doyle, Jr. (D)
- Lieutenant Governor: Barbara Lawton (D)
- Attorney General: J.B. Van Hollen (R)
- Secretary of State: Douglas LaFollette (D)
- Treasurer: Dawn Marie Sass (D)
- State Superintendent of Public Instruction (Non-partisan Office): Tony Evers

See also:

- Wisconsin Constitution
- Governors of Wisconsin
- Wisconsin State Legislature
  - Wisconsin State Senate
  - Wisconsin State Assembly
- Wisconsin Supreme Court
- U.S. Congressional Delegations from Wisconsin
- Map of congressional districts
- List of U.S. Senators from Wisconsin

The Wisconsin State Capitol

Politics

Presidential elections results

Year	Republican	Democratic
2008	42.31% *1,262,393*	**56.22%** *1,677,211*
2004	49.31% *1,478,120*	**49.71%** *1,489,504*
2000	47.56% *1,237,279*	**47.83%** *1,242,987*
1996	38.48% *845,029*	**48.81%** *1,071,971*
1992	36.78% *930,855*	**41.13%** *1,041,066*

| 1988 | 47.80% *1,047,794* | **51.41%** *1,126,794* |

During the period of the Civil War, Wisconsin was a Republican and pro-Union stronghold. Ethno-religious issues in the late 19th century caused a brief split in the Republican coalition. Through the first half of the 20th century, Wisconsin's politics were dominated by Robert La Follette and his sons, originally of the Republican Party, but later of the revived Progressive Party. Since 1945, the state has maintained a close balance between Republicans and Democrats. Republican Senator Joe McCarthy was a controversial national figure in the early 1950s. Recent leading Republicans include former Governor Tommy Thompson and Congressman F. James Sensenbrenner, Jr.; prominent Democrats include Senators Herb Kohl and Russ Feingold, and Congressman David Obey.

Much of the state's political history involved coalitions among different ethnic groups. The most famous controversy dealt with foreign language teaching in schools. This was fought out in the Bennett Law campaign of 1890, when the Germans switched to the Democratic Party because of the Republican Party's support of the Bennett Law, which led to a major victory for the Democrats.

The cities of Wisconsin have been active in increasing the availability of legislative information on the internet, thereby providing for greater government transparency. Currently three of the five most populous cities in Wisconsin provide their constituents with internet based access of all public records directly from the cities' databases. Wisconsin cities started to make this a priority after Milwaukee began doing so, on their page [3], in 2001. One such city, Madison, has been named the Number 1 digital city by the Center for Digital Government [4] in consecutive years. Nearly 18 percent of Wisconsin's population has the ability to access their municipality's information in this way.

Wisconsin has voted for the Democratic presidential nominee in the last six elections. The urban centers of Milwaukee and Madison tend to vote strongly Democratic. The suburbs of those cities are politically diverse, but tend to vote Republican. Counties in the western part of the state tend to be liberal, a tradition passed down from Scandinavian immigrants. The rural areas in the northern and eastern part of the state are the most solidly Republican areas in Wisconsin.[*citation needed*]

In the 2008 presidential election, Wisconsin voted for the Democratic presidential nominee, Illinois Senator Barack Obama. Obama captured 56% of the vote statewide, with the urban centers of Milwaukee and Madison voting strongly Democratic. Bucking the historic trend, Brown County (home to Green Bay) and Outagamie County (home to Appleton) voted for Obama over John McCain, the Republican presidential nominee. In all, McCain captured approximately 42% of the vote statewide and won 13 of the state's 72 counties. Of the counties won by McCain, only a handful were by greater than 55% of the vote (Florence, Green Lake, Ozaukee, Washington, and Waukesha, with Washington County providing his largest single-county percentage victory in the state). In all, Obama was successful in 59 counties, transcending the state's usual east/west and urban/suburban/rural divides.

Wisconsin ranked second in voter turnout in the 2008 presidential election, behind Minnesota.

Further information: Political party strength in Wisconsin

Lawmakers in Wisconsin

The last election in which Wisconsin supported a Republican Presidential candidate was in 1984. However, both the 2000 and 2004 presidential elections were close, with Wisconsin receiving heavy doses of national advertising because it was a "swing," or pivot, state. Al Gore carried the presidential vote in 2000 by only 5,700 votes, and John Kerry won Wisconsin in 2004 by 11,000 votes. However, in 2008, Barack Obama carried the state by 381,000 votes and with 56%. Republicans had a stronghold in the Fox Valley but elected a Democrat, Steve Kagen, of Appleton, for the 8th Congressional District in 2006. Republicans have held Waukesha County. The City of Milwaukee heads the list of Wisconsin's Democratic strongholds, which also includes Madison and the state's Native American reservations. Wisconsin's largest Congressional district, the 7th, has been a Democratic stronghold since 1969. Its representative, David Obey, chairs the powerful House Appropriations Committee.

- Wisconsin's political history encompasses, on the one hand, "Fighting Bob" La Follette and the Progressive movement; and on the other, Joe McCarthy, the controversial anti-Communist censured by the Senate during the 1950s.
- In the early 20th century, the Socialist Party of America had a base in Milwaukee. The phenomenon was referred to as "sewer socialism" because the elected officials were more concerned with public works and reform than with revolution (although revolutionary socialism existed in the city as well). Its influence faded in the late 1950s, largely because of the red scare and racial tensions. The first Socialist mayor of a large city in the United States was Emil Seidel, elected mayor of Milwaukee in 1910; another Socialist, Daniel Hoan, was mayor of Milwaukee from 1916 to 1940; and a third, Frank P. Zeidler, from 1948–1960. Socialist newspaper editor Victor Berger was repeatedly elected as a U.S. Representative, although he was prevented from serving for some time because of his opposition to the First World War.
- William Proxmire, a Democratic Senator (1957–89) dominated the Democratic party for years; he was best known for attacking waste and fraud in federal spending.
- Democrat Russ Feingold was the only Senator to vote against the Patriot Act in 2001.
- Democrat Tammy Baldwin from Madison was the first, and is currently the only, openly lesbian U.S. Representative.
- In 2004, Gwen Moore, a Democrat from Milwaukee, became Wisconsin's first African-American U.S. Representative.

In 2006, Democrats gained in a national sweep of opposition to the Bush administration, and the Iraq War. The retiring GOP 8th District Congressman, Mark Green, of Green Bay, ran against the incumbent Governor Jim Doyle. Green lost by 8% statewide, making Doyle the first Democratic Governor to be re-elected in 32 years. The Republicans lost control of the state Senate. Although Democrats gained eight seats in the state Assembly, Republicans retained a five vote majority in that house. In 2008, Democrats regained control of the State Assembly by a 52–46 margin, marking the first time since 1987 the both the governor and state legislature were both Democratic.

Taxes

Wisconsin collects personal income taxes (based on five income brackets) which range from 4.6% to 7.75%. The state sales and use tax rate is 5.0%. Fifty-nine counties have an additional sales/use tax of 0.5%. Milwaukee County and four surrounding counties have an additional temporary 0.1% tax which helps fund the Miller Park baseball stadium, which was completed in 2001. Retailers who make sales subject to applicable county taxes must collect this tax on their retail sales.

The most common property tax assessed on Wisconsin residents is the real property tax, or their residential property tax. Wisconsin does not impose a property tax on vehicles, but does levy an annual registration fee. Property taxes are the most important tax revenue source for Wisconsin's local governments, as well as major methods of funding school districts, vocational technical colleges, special purpose districts and tax incremental finance districts. Equalized values are based on the full market value of all taxable property in the state, except for agricultural land. In order to provide property tax relief for farmers, the value of agricultural land is determined by its value for agricultural uses, rather than for its possible development value. Equalized values are used to distribute state aid payments to counties, municipalities, and technical colleges. Assessments prepared by local assessors are used to distribute the property tax burden within individual municipalities.

Wisconsin does not assess a tax on intangible property. Wisconsin does not collect inheritance taxes. Until January 1, 2008 Wisconsin's estate tax was decoupled from the federal estate tax laws; therefore the state imposed its own estate tax on certain large estates.

There are no toll roads in Wisconsin; highway and road construction and maintenance is funded by motor fuel tax revenues.

Economy

In 2008 Wisconsin's gross state product was $240.4 billion, making it 21st among U.S. states. The per capita personal income was $35,239 in 2008. The economy of Wisconsin is driven by manufacturing, agriculture, and health care. Although manufacturing accounts for a far greater part of the state's income than farming, Wisconsin is often perceived as a farming state.

As of June 2010, the states unemployment rate is 7.9% (seasonally adjusted)

The US Bank Center in Milwaukee is Wisconsin's tallest skyscraper.

In October 2010, the largest employers in Wisconsin were:

1. Wal-Mart
2. University of Wisconsin-Madison
3. Milwaukee Public Schools
4. U.S. Postal Service
5. Wisconsin Department of Corrections
6. Menards
7. Marshfield Clinic
8. Aurora Health Care
9. City of Milwaukee
10. Wisconsin Department of Veterans Affairs

Agriculture

Wisconsin is second to California in in overall production of milk and butter, and third in per-capita milk production, behind Idaho and Vermont, though it leads the nation in cheese production. Wisconsin ranks first nationally in the production of corn for silage, cranberries, ginseng, and snap beans for processing. Wisconsin is also a leading producer of oats, potatoes, carrots, tart cherries, maple syrup, and sweet corn for processing. The importance of the state's agricultural production was exemplified by the depiction of a Holstein cow, an ear of corn, and a wheel of cheese for Wisconsin's 50 State Quarters design.

A large part of the state's manufacturing sector includes commercial food processing, including well-known brands such as Oscar Mayer, Tombstone frozen pizza, Johnsonville brats, and Usinger's sausage. Kraft Foods alone employs over 5,000 people in the state. Milwaukee is a major producer of beer and was formerly headquarters for Miller Brewing Company, the nation's second-largest brewer, until it merged with Coors Brewing Company. Formerly, Schlitz, Blatz, and Pabst were cornerstone breweries in Milwaukee.

Badger State	
State Animal:	Badger
State Domesticated Animal:	Dairy cow
State Wild Animal:	White-tailed deer
State Beverage:	Milk
State Fruit:	Cranberry
State Bird:	Robin
State Capital:	Madison
State Dog:	American water spaniel
State Fish:	Muskellunge
State Flower:	Wood violet
State Fossil:	Trilobite
State Grain:	Corn
State Insect:	European honey bee
State Motto:	*Forward*
State Song:	"On, Wisconsin!"
State Tree:	Sugar maple
State Mineral:	Galena (Lead sulfide)
State Rock:	Red granite
State Soil:	Antigo silt loam
State Dance:	Polka
State Symbol of Peace:	Mourning dove
State Microbe	Lactococcus lactis

Manufacturing

Wisconsin is home to a very large and diversified manufacturing economy, with special focus on transportation and capital equipment. Major Wisconsin companies in these categories include the Kohler Company, Mercury Marine, Rockwell Automation, Johnson Controls, Seagrave Fire Apparatus, Pierce Manufacturing(fire apparatus), Briggs & Stratton, Miller Electric, Milwaukee Electric Tool Company, Bucyrus International, Joy Global Inc., The Manitowoc Company, Super Steel Products Corp., Ladish Co., Oshkosh Truck, and Harley-Davidson.

Consumer goods

Wisconsin is a major producer of paper, packaging, and other consumer goods. Major consumer products companies based in the state include SC Johnson & Co., and Diversey Inc., Wisconsin also ranks first nationwide in the production of paper products; the lower Fox River from Lake Winnebago to Green Bay has 24 paper mills along its 39 miles (63 km) stretch.

The development and manufacture of health care devices and software is a growing sector of the state's economy with key players such as GE Healthcare, Epic Systems, and TomoTherapy.

Tourism

Tourism is also a major industry in Wisconsin – the state's third largest, according to the Department of Tourism. This is attributed to the many resorts in northern Wisconsin and the family attractions in the Wisconsin Dells area, which attract nearly 3 million visitors per year.[*citation needed*] Tourist destinations such as the House on the Rock near Spring Green and Circus World Museum in Baraboo also draw thousands of visitors annually, and festivals such as Summerfest and the EAA Oshkosh Airshow draw international attention, along with hundreds of thousands of visitors.

Given the large number of lakes and rivers in the state, water recreation is very popular.

The distinctive Door Peninsula, which extends off the eastern coast of the state, contains one of the state's tourist destinations, Door County. Door County is a popular destination for boaters because of the large number of natural harbors, bays and ports on the Green Bay and Lake Michigan side of the peninsula that forms the county. The area draws hundreds of thousands of visitors yearly to its quaint villages, seasonal cherry picking, and fish boils.

Film industry

On January 1, 2008, a new tax incentive for the film industry came into effect. The first major production to take advantage of the tax incentive was Michael Mann's *Public Enemies*. While the producers spent $18 million dollars on the film, it was reported that most of that went to out-of-state workers and for out-of-state services; Wisconsin taxpayers had provided $4.6 million in subsidies, and derived only $5 million in revenues from the film's making.

Important municipalities

Wisconsin's self-promotion as "America's Dairyland" sometimes leads to a mistaken impression that it is an exclusively rural state. However, Wisconsin contains cities and towns of all sizes. Over 68% of Wisconsin residents live in urban areas, with the Greater Milwaukee area home to roughly one-third of the state's population. Milwaukee is at the northern edge of an urban area bordering Lake Michigan that stretches southward into greater Chicago and northwestern Indiana, with a population of over 11 million. With over 602,000 residents Milwaukee proper is the 22nd-largest city in the country. The string of cities along the western edge of Lake Michigan is generally considered to be an example of a megalopolis. Madison's dual identity as state capital and college town gives it a cultural richness unusual in a city its size. With a population of around 220,000, and metropolitan area of over 600,000, Madison is also a very fast-growing city. Madison's suburb, Middleton, was also ranked the "Best Place to Live in America" in 2007 by *Money Magazine*. Medium-size cities dot the state and anchor a network of working farms surrounding them. As of 2007, there were 12 cities in Wisconsin with a population of 50,000 or more. Cities and villages are incorporated urban areas in Wisconsin. Towns are unincorporated minor civil divisions of counties.

Wisconsin counties

Further information: List of municipalities in Wisconsin by population and Political subdivisions of Wisconsin

Appleton

Eau Claire

Janesville

Kenosha

La Crosse

Madison

Milwaukee

Oshkosh

Racine

Education

Wisconsin, along with Minnesota and Michigan, was among the Midwestern leaders in the emergent American state university movement following the Civil War in the United States. By the turn of the century, education in the state advocated the "Wisconsin Idea", which emphasized for service to the people of the state. The "Wisconsin Idea" exemplified the Progressive movement within colleges and universities at the time. Today, public education in Wisconsin includes both the 26-campus University of Wisconsin System, with the flagship university University of Wisconsin–Madison, and the 16-campus Wisconsin Technical College System which coordinates with the University of Wisconsin. Notable private colleges and universities include Marquette University, Milwaukee School of Engineering, Medical College of Wisconsin, Concordia University Wisconsin, Carroll University, Edgewood College, Beloit College, St. Norbert College, Lakeland College, Cardinal Stritch University and Lawrence University, among others. Elementary, middle and high school education are mandatory by law.

See also: List of colleges and universities in Wisconsin

See also: List of high schools in Wisconsin

See also: List of school districts in Wisconsin

Culture

Citizens of Wisconsin are referred to as Wisconsinites. The traditional prominence of references to dairy farming and cheesemaking in Wisconsin's rural economy (the state's license plates have read "America's Dairyland" since 1940) have led to the nickname (sometimes used pejoratively among non-residents) of "cheeseheads" and to the creation of "cheesehead hats" made of yellow foam in the shape of a block of cheese.

Numerous ethnic festivals are held throughout Wisconsin to celebrate its heritage. Such festivals include Summerfest, Oktoberfest, German Fest, Festa Italiana, Irish Fest, Bastille Days, Syttende Mai (Norwegian Constitution Day), Brat(wurst) Days in Sheboygan, Cheese Days in Monroe and Mequon, African World Festival, Indian Summer, Arab Fest, and many others.

Art

The Milwaukee Art Museum in Milwaukee, designed by Santiago Calatrava, is known for its interesting architecture. The Milwaukee County Zoological Gardens cover over 200 acres (0.81 km^2) of land on the far west side of the city. Madison is home to the Vilas Zoo which is free for all visitors, and the Olbrich Gardens conservatory, as well as the hub of cultural activity at the University of Wisconsin–Madison. It is also known for Monona Terrace, a convention center that was designed by Taliesin Architect Anthony Puttnam, based loosely on a 1930s design by Frank Lloyd Wright, a world-renowned architect and Wisconsin native who was born in Richland Center. Wright's home and studio in the 20th century was at Taliesin, south of Spring Green. Decades after Wright's death, Taliesin remains an architectural office and school for his followers.

The Milwaukee Art Museum

Frank Lloyd Wright's Taliesin in Spring Green, Wisconsin

Music

Main article: Music of Wisconsin

Wisconsin has more country music festivals than any other state,[citation needed] including Miller Lite Presents Country Fest, Bud Light Presents Country Jam USA, the Coors Hodag Country Festival, Porterfield Country Music Festival, Country Thunder USA in Twin Lakes, Log Jam Fest in Phillips and Ford Presents Country USA.

The state's largest city, Milwaukee, also hosts Summerfest, dubbed "The World's Largest Music Festival," every year. This festival is held at the lakefront Henry Maier Festival Park just south of downtown.

Wisconsin has both the Milwaukee Metalfest and the Northern Wisconsin Metalfest, which is held in Lake Nebagamon.

The Wisconsin Area Music Industry provides an annual WAMI event where it presents an awards show for top Wisconsin artists.

Alcohol and Wisconsin culture

Music stage at Summerfest in 1994, currently called the Harley-Davidson Roadhouse, with Downtown Milwaukee and an approach to the Hoan Bridge in the background.

The Wisconsin Tavern League is a strong political force and the state legislature has been reluctant to lower DUI offense from BAC 0.10 to 0.08 (only through Federal government influence) and raise the alcoholic beverage tax. The *Milwaukee Journal Sentinel* series "Wasted in Wisconsin" examined this situation. Popular belief is that the state's large German heritage population, climate (long cold winters, short warm summers), and abundant leisure opportunities contribute to high drinking rates, though data collected by the *Journal Sentinel* do not conclusively support this.[citation needed]

Recreation

The varied landscape of Wisconsin makes the state a popular vacation destination for outdoor recreation. Winter events include skiing, ice fishing and snowmobile derbies. Wisconsin has many lakes of varied size; the state contains 11188 square miles (28980 km^2) of water, more than all but three other states (Alaska, Michigan and Florida).

Outdoor activities are popular in Wisconsin, especially hunting and fishing. One of the most prevalent game animals is the whitetail deer. Each year in Wisconsin, well over 600,000 deer hunting licenses are sold. In 2008, the Wisconsin Department of Natural Resources projected the pre-hunt deer population to be about 1.5 to 1.7 million.

Sports

Main article: Sports in Wisconsin

Wisconsin is represented by major league teams in three sports: football, baseball, and basketball. Lambeau Field, located in Green Bay, Wisconsin is home to the National Football League's Green Bay Packers. The

Lambeau Field in Green Bay is home to the NFL's Green Bay Packers.

Packers have been part of the NFL since the league's second season in 1921 and hold the record for the most NFL titles, earning the city of Green Bay the nickname "Titletown USA". The Packers are the smallest city franchise in the NFL, and are the only one owned by the people of the city.. The franchise was founded by "Curly" Lambeau who played and coached for them. The Green Bay Packers are one of the most successful small-market professional sports franchises in the world and have won 12 NFL championships, including the first two AFL-NFL Championship games (Super Bowls I and II) and Super Bowl XXXI. The state's support of the team is evidenced by the 81,000-person waiting list for season tickets to Lambeau Field.

Miller Park is the home stadium of Major League Baseball's Milwaukee Brewers

The Milwaukee Brewers, the state's only major league baseball team, play in Miller Park in Milwaukee, the successor to Milwaukee County Stadium since 2001. In 1982, the Brewers won the American League Championship, marking their most successful season. The team switched from the American League to the National League starting with the 1998 season.

The Milwaukee Bucks of the National Basketball Association play home games at the Bradley Center. The Bucks won the NBA Championship in 1971.

The state also has minor league teams in hockey (Milwaukee Admirals and Madison Ice Muskies) and baseball (the Wisconsin Timber Rattlers, based in Appleton and the Beloit Snappers of the Class A minor leagues). Wisconsin is also home to the Madison Mallards, the La Crosse Loggers, the Eau Claire Express, the Green Bay Bullfrogs, the Wisconsin Woodchucks, and the Wisconsin Rapids Rafters of the Northwoods League, a collegiate all-star summer league. In arena football Wisconsin is represented by four teams: the Wisconsin Wolfpack in Madison and the Milwaukee Bonecrushers, both in the CIFL; the Green Bay Blizzard of the IFL, and the Milwaukee Iron of the AFL.

Wisconsin also has many college sports programs, including the Wisconsin Badgers, of the University of Wisconsin–Madison. The Wisconsin Badgers football former head coach Barry Alvarez led the

Badgers to three Rose Bowl championships, including back-to-back victories in 1999 and 2000. The Badger men's basketball team won the national title in 1941 and made a second trip to college basketball's Final Four in 2000. The Badgers claimed a historic dual championship in 2006 when both the women's and men's hockey teams won national titles.

The Marquette Golden Eagles of the Big East Conference, the state's other major collegiate program, is known for its men's basketball team, which, under the direction of Al McGuire, won the NCAA National Championship in 1977. The team returned to the Final Four in 2003.

The Semi-Professional Northern Elite Football League consists of many teams from Wisconsin. The league is made up of former professional, collegiate, and high school players. Teams from Wisconsin include: The Green Bay Gladiators from Green Bay, WI, The Fox Valley Force in Appleton, WI, The Kimberly Storm in Kimberly, WI, The Central Wisconsin Spartans in Wausau, WI, The Eau Claire Crush and the Chippewa Valley Predators from Eau Claire, WI, and the Superior Stampede from Superior, WI. The league also has teams in Michigan and Minnesota. Teams play from May until August.

Wisconsin is home to the world's oldest operational racetrack. The Milwaukee Mile, located in State Fair Park in West Allis held races there long before the Indy 500.

Wisconsin is home to the nation's oldest operating velodrome in Kenosha where races have been held every year since 1927.

See also

Main articles: Outline of Wisconsin and Index of Wisconsin-related articles

Further reading

- Barone, Michael; Cohen, Richard E. (2005). *The Almanac of American Politics, 2006*. Washington, DC: National Journal. ISBN 0892341122.
- Current, Richard (2001). *Wisconsin: A History*. Urbana: University of Illinois Press. ISBN 0252070186.
- Gara, Larry (1962). *A Short History of Wisconsin*. Madison: State Historical Society of Wisconsin.
- Holmes, Fred L. (1946). *Wisconsin*. 5 vols. Chicago. Detailed popular history and many biographies.
- Nesbit, Robert C. (1989). *Wisconsin: A History* (Rev. ed.). Madison: University of Wisconsin Press. ISBN 0299108007.
- Pearce, Neil (1980). *The Great Lakes States of America*. New York: Norton. ISBN 0393056198.
- Quaife, Milo M. (1924). *Wisconsin, Its History and Its People, 1634–1924*. 4 vols. Detailed popular history & biographies.
- Raney, William Francis (1940). *Wisconsin: A Story of Progress*. New York: Prentice-Hall.

- Robinson, Arthur H.; Culver, J. B., eds (1974). *The Atlas of Wisconsin*.
- Sisson, Richard, ed (2006). *The American Midwest: An Interpretive Encyclopedia*. Bloomington: Indiana University Press. ISBN 0253348862.
- Vogeler, I. (1986). *Wisconsin: A Geography*. Boulder: Westview Press. ISBN 0865314926.
- Wisconsin Cartographers' Guild (2002). *Wisconsin's Past and Present: A Historical Atlas*.
- Works Progress Administration (1941). *Wisconsin: A Guide to the Badger State*. Detailed guide to every town and city, and cultural history.

   See additional books at History of Wisconsin

External links

- Map of Wisconsin at nationalatlas.gov [5]
- U.S. Census Bureau [6]
- State of Wisconsin [7]
- Wisconsin state symbols [8]
- Wisconsin State Legislature [9]
- Wisconsin Court System [10]
- Wisconsin State Facts [11]
- Wisconsin Health and Demographic Data [12]
- Energy Profile for Wisconsin- Economic, environmental, and energy data [13]
- Wisconsin Historical Society [14]
- Wisconsin's Name: Where It Came From and What It Means [15]
- The State of Wisconsin Collection [16] from the UW Digital Collections Center [17]
- Wisconsin Historical Images [18]
- Wisconsin Free Speech Legacy [19]
- Misspronouncer [20], a pronunciation guide for everything Wisconsin.
- Wisconsin Department of Tourism [21]
- Wisconsinology Blog [22]
- Wisconsin travel guide from Wikitravel
- Wisconsin Hotels [23]
- Wisconsin [24] at the Open Directory Project

Geographical coordinates: 44°30′N 89°30′W

frr:Wisconsin pnb:وسکونسن

History

Ojibwe language

Ojibwe language	
Anishinaabemowin, ᐊᓂᔑᓇᐯᒧᐎᓐ	
Pronunciation	[anɪʃinaːpeːmowɪn]
Spoken in	Canada, United States
Region	Canada: Quebec, Ontario, Manitoba, Saskatchewan, groups in Alberta, British Columbia; United States: Michigan, Wisconsin, Minnesota, groups in North Dakota, Montana
Total speakers	56,531 (47,740 in Canada; 8,791 in the United States)

Language family	Algic
	• Algonquian
	  • Central Algonquian
	    • Ojibwe language

Writing system	Latin alphabet, various orthographies in Canada and the United States; Ojibwe syllabics in Canada; Great Lakes Algonquian syllabary in the United States
Language codes	
ISO 639-1	`oj`
ISO 639-2	`oji`
ISO 639-3	variously: `alq`[1] – Algonquin `ojs`[2] – Severn Ojibwa `ojg`[3] – Eastern Ojibwa `ojc`[4] – Central Ojibwa `ojb`[5] – Northwestern Ojibwa `ojw`[6] – Western Ojibwa `ciw`[7] – Chippewa `otw`[8] – Ottawa
Linguasphere	

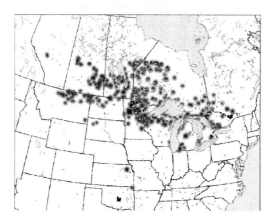

Location of all Ojibwe Reservations/Reserves and cities with an Ojibwe population in North America, with diffusion rings about communities speaking the Ojibwe language

This article contains IPA phonetic symbols. Without proper rendering support, you may see question marks, boxes, or other symbols instead of Unicode characters.

This article contains Canadian Aboriginal syllabic characters. Without proper rendering support, you may see question marks, boxes, or other symbols instead of syllabics.

Ojibwe (or **Ojibwa**, **Ojibway**, **Chippewa**), also called Anishinaabe, is an indigenous language of the Algonquian linguistic family. Ojibwe is characterized by a series of dialects that have local names and frequently local (non-indigenous) writing systems. There is no single dialect that is considered the most prestigious or most prominent, and no standard writing system that covers all dialects. The relative autonomy of the regional dialects of Ojibwe is associated with an absence of linguistic or political unity among Ojibwe-speaking groups.

The dialects of Ojibwe are spoken in Canada from southwestern Quebec, through Ontario, Manitoba and parts of Saskatchewan, with outlying communities in Alberta, and in the United States from Michigan through Wisconsin and Minnesota, with a number of communities in North Dakota and Montana, as well as migrant groups in Kansas and Oklahoma.

The aggregated dialects of Ojibwe comprise the second most commonly spoken First Nations language in Canada (after Cree), and the fourth most widely spoken in the United States or Canada behind Navajo, Inuit and Cree.

Classification

The Algonquian language family of which Ojibwe is a member is itself a member of the Algic language family, other Algic languages being Wiyot and Yurok. Ojibwe is sometimes described as a Central Algonquian language, along with Fox, Cree, Menominee, Miami-Illinois, Potawatomi, and Shawnee. Central Algonquian is a geographical term of convenience rather than a genetic subgroup, and its use does not indicate that the Central languages are more closely related to each other than to the other Algonquian languages.

Exonyms and endonyms

The most general indigenous designation for the language is *Anishinaabemowin* 'speaking the native language' (*Anishinaabe* 'native person,' verb suffix *–mo* 'speak a language,' suffix *–win* 'nominalizer'), with varying spellings and pronunciations depending upon dialect. Some speakers use the term *Ojibwemowin*. The general term in the Severn Ojibwe dialect is *Anihshininiimowin*, although *Anishinaabemowin* is widely recognized by Severn speakers. Some speakers of Saulteaux Ojibwe refer to their language as *Nakawemowin*. The Ottawa dialect is sometimes referred to as *Daawaamwin*, although the general designation is *Nishnaabemwin*, with the latter term also applied to *Jibwemwin* or Eastern Ojibwe. Other local terms are listed in Ojibwe dialects. English terms include *Ojibwe*, with variants including *Ojibwa* and *Ojibway*. The related term *Chippewa* is more commonly employed in the United States and in southwestern Ontario among descendants of Ojibwe migrants from the United States.

Relationship of Ojibwe and Potawatomi

Ojibwe and Potawatomi are frequently viewed as being more closely related to each than to other Algonquian languages. Ojibwe and Potawatomi have been proposed as likely candidates for forming a genetic subgroup within Proto-Algonquian, although the required research to ascertain the linguistic history and status of a hypothetical "Ojibwe-Potawatomi" subgroup has not yet been undertaken. A discussion of Algonquian family subgroups indicates that "Ojibwe-Potawatomi is another possibility that awaits investigation." In a proposed consensus classification of Algonquian languages, Goddard (1996) classifies Ojibwa and Potawatomi as "Ojibwayan," although no supporting evidence is adduced.

The Central languages share a significant number of common features. These features can generally attributed to diffusion of features through borrowing: "Extensive lexical, phonological, and perhaps grammatical borrowing—the diffusion of elements and features across language boundaries—appears to have been the major factor in giving the languages in the area of the Upper Great Lakes their generally similar cast, and it has not been possible to find any shared innovations substantial enough to require the postulation of a genetically distinct Central Algonquian subgroup."

The possibility that the proposed genetic subgrouping of Ojibwa and Potawatomi can also be accounted for as diffusion has also been raised: "The putative Ojibwa-Potawatomi subgroup is similarly open to question, but cannot be evaluated without more information on Potawatomi dialects."

Geographic distribution

Pre-contact distribution of the Plains Ojibwe, Southwestern Ojibwe (Chippewa), and Algonquin dialects of the Ojibwe language

Ojibwe communities are found in Canada from southwestern Quebec, through Ontario, southern Manitoba and parts of southern Saskatchewan, and in the United States from northern Michigan through northern Wisconsin and northern Minnesota, with a number of communities in northern North Dakota and northern Montana. Groups of speakers of the Ottawa dialect migrated to Kansas and Oklahoma during the historical period, with a small amount of linguistic documentation of the language in Oklahoma. The presence of Ojibwe in British Columbia has been noted.

Current census data indicate that all varieties of Ojibwe are spoken by approximately 56,531 people. This figure reflects census data from the 2000 United States census and the 2006 Canadian census. The Ojibwe language is reported as spoken by 8,791 total people in the United States of which 7,355 are Native Americans and by as many as 47,740 in Canada, making it one of the largest Algic languages by numbers of speakers.

Language	Canada	United States	Total (by speakers)	Total ethnic population
Algonquin	2,680	0	2,680	8,266
Oji-Cree	12,600	0	12,600	12,600
Ojibwe	24,896	8,355	33,251	219,711
Ottawa	7,564	436	8,000	60,000
Total (by Country)	47,740	8,791	**56,531**	300,577

Dialects

Main article: Ojibwe dialects

Because the dialects of Ojibwe are at least partly mutually intelligible, Ojibwe is usually considered to be a single language with a number of dialects, i.e. Ojibwe is "...conventionally regarded as a single language consisting of a continuum of dialectal varieties since ... every dialect is at least partly intelligible to the speakers of the neighboring dialects." The degree of mutually intelligibility between nonadjacent dialects varies considerably; recent research has shown that there is strong differentiation between the Ottawa dialect spoken in southern Ontario and northern Michigan; the Severn Ojibwa dialect spoken in northern Ontario and Manitoba; and the Algonquin dialect spoken in southwestern Quebec. Valentine notes that these three dialects "...show many distinct features, which suggest periods of relative isolation from other varieties of Ojibwe." Many communities adjacent to these relatively sharply differentiated dialects show a mix of transitional features, reflecting overlap with other nearby dialects. While each of these dialects has undergone innovations that make them distinctive, their status as part of the Ojibwe language complex is not in dispute. The relatively low degrees of mutual intelligibility between some nonadjacent Ojibwe dialects led Rhodes and Todd to suggest that Ojibwe "...could be said to consist of several languages...," suggesting analysis of Ojibwe as a linguistic subgroup.

While there is some variation in the classification of Ojibwe dialects, at a minimum the following are recognized, proceeding west to east: Western Ojibwe (Saulteaux), Southwestern Ojibwe (Chippewa), Northwestern Ojibwe, Severn Ojibwe (Oji-Cree), Ottawa (Odawa), Eastern Ojibwe, and Algonquin. Based upon contemporary field research, Valentine also recognizes several other dialects: Berens Ojibwe in northwestern Ontario, which he distinguishes from Northwestern Ojibwe; North of (Lake) Superior; and Nipissing. The latter two cover approximately the same territory as Central Ojibwa, which he does not recognize.

Two recent analyses of the relationships between the Ojibwe dialects are in agreement on the assignment of the strongly differentiated Ottawa dialect to a separate subgroup, and the assignment of Severn Ojibwe and Algonquin to another subgroup, and differ primarily with respect to the relationships between the less strongly differentiated dialects. Rhodes and Todd recognize several different dialectal subgroupings within Ojibwe: (a) Ottawa; (b) Severn and Algonquian; (c) a third subgroup which is further divided into (i) a subgrouping of Northwestern Ojibwe and Saulteaux, and a subgrouping consisting of Eastern Ojibwe and a further subgrouping comprising Southwestern Ojibwe and Central Ojibwe. Valentine has proposed that Ojibwe dialects are divided into three groups: a northern tier consisting of Severn Ojibwe and Algonquin; a southern tier consisting of "Odawa, Chippewa, Eastern Ojibwe, the Ojibwe of the Border Lakes region between Minnesota and Ontario, and Saulteaux; and third, a transitional zone between these two polar groups, in which there is a mixture of northern and southern features."

Lingua franca

Several different Ojibwe dialects have functioned as lingua franca or trade languages in the circum-Great Lakes area, particularly in interactions with speakers of other Algonquian languages. Documentation of such usage dates from the 18th and 19th centuries, but earlier use is likely, with reports as early as 1703 suggesting that Ojibwe was used by different groups from the Gulf of Saint Lawrence to Lake Winnipeg, and from as far south as Ohio to Hudson Bay.

A sign at Lakehead University in English and Anishinaabemowin.

A trade language is "...a language customarily used for communication between speakers of different languages, even though it may be that neither speaker has the trade language as his dominant language..." although "...there is a relatively high degree of bilingualism involving the trade language."

Documentation from the 17th century indicates that Huron (also called Wyandot), an Iroquoian language, was also used as a trade language east of the Great Lakes by speakers of the Nipissing and Algonquin dialects of Ojibwe, and also by other groups south of the Great Lakes, including the Winnebago and by a group of unknown affiliation identified only as "Assistaeronon." The political decline of the Hurons in the 18th century and the ascendancy of Ojibwe-speaking groups including the Ottawa led to the replacement of Huron as a lingua franca.

In the area east of Georgian Bay, the Nipissing dialect was a trade language. In the Lower Peninsula of Michigan, the eastern end of the Upper Peninsula, the area between Lake Erie and Lake Huron, and along the north shore of Georgian Bay, the Ottawa dialect served as a trade language. In the area south of Lake Superior and west of Lake Michigan Southwestern Ojibwe was the trade language. A widespread pattern of asymmetrical bilingualism is found in the area south of the Great Lakes, in which speakers of Potawatomi or Menominee, both Algonquian languages, could also speak Ojibwe, but Ojibwe speakers did not speak the other languages. It is known that some speakers of Menominee also speak Ojibwe, and that this pattern persisted into the 20th century. Similarly bilingualism in Ojibwe is still common among Potawatomis who speak Potawatomi.

Reports from traders and travellers as early as 1744 indicated that speakers of Menominee, another Algonquian language, used Ojibwe as a lingua franca. Other reports from the 18th century and early

19th century indicate that speakers of the unrelated Siouan language Ho-Chunk (Winnebago) also used Ojibwe when dealing with Europeans and others. Other reports indicate that agents of the American government at Green Bay, Wisconsin spoke Ojibwe in their interactions with Menominee, with other reports indicating that "…the Chippewa, Menominee, Ottawa, Potawatomi, Sac, and Fox tribes used Ojibwe in intertribal communication…" Some reports indicate that further to the west speakers of non-Algonquian languages such as Ho-Chunk (Winnebago), Iowa, and Pawnee spoke Ojibwe as an 'acquired language.'

Broken Oghibbeway

During the fur trade era, a pidgin form of Ojibwe known as *Broken Oghibbeway* was used by travellers and traders in the Wisconsin and Mississippi River valleys. Data in the language were collected during the 1820s at Prairie du Chien, Wisconsin by Edwin James, a physician and naturalist, who also gave the pidgin its name. It has been described as "…a language with a restricted vocabulary drawn from the Ottawa dialect of Ojibwe with a few words from Fox (Mesquakie), another Algonquian language of the region, and restructured and reduced, but not absent, Ojibwe morphology."

James recognized that "Broken Oghibbeway" was different from the variety of Ojibwe spoken in Wisconsin (which at that time included Minnesota). He noted that it "…is of the dialect used by the traders and the people of mixed blood in speaking with the Menomonies and Winnebagoes also many of the Sioux Saxes and Foxes."

Although "Broken Oghibbeway" retains many aspects of the complex inflectional morphology that characterizes Ojibwe, it is nonetheless simplified and restructured, with reductions in the treatment of transitivity and gender, with simplification of the system of personal prefixes used on verbs, loss of the negative suffix that occurs on verbs, and loss of inflectional suffixes that indicate grammatical objects.

Ojibwe influence on other languages

Michif is a mixed language that primarily is based upon French and Plains Cree, with some vocabulary from Ojibwe, in addition to phonological influence in Michif-speaking communities where there is a significant Ojibwe influence. In locations such as Turtle Mountain, North Dakota individuals of Ojibwe ancestry now speak only Michif and not Ojibwe.

Ojibwe borrowings have been noted in Menominee, a related Algonquian language.

Bungee is the name given to a dialect of English spoken in Manitoba by the descendants of "English, Scottish, and Orkney fur traders and their Cree or Saulteaux wives…". Bungee incorporates elements of Cree; the name may be from the Ojibwe word *bangii* 'a little bit' or the Cree equivalent but whether there is any other Ojibwe component in Bungee is not documented.

Phonology

Main article: Ojibwe phonology

All dialects of Ojibwe generally have an inventory of seventeen consonants. Most dialects have the segment glottal stop /ʔ/ in their inventory of consonant phonemes; Severn Ojibwe and the Algonquin dialect have /h/ in its place. Some dialects have both segments phonetically, but only one is present in phonological representations. The Ottawa and Southwestern Ojibwe (Chippewa) have /h/ in a small number of affective vocabulary items in addition to regular /ʔ/. Some dialects may have otherwise non-occurring sounds such as /f, l, r/ in loanwords.

Obstruent consonants are divided into lenis and fortis sets, with these features having varying phonological analyses and phonetic realizations cross-dialectally. In some dialects, such as Severn Ojibwe, members of the fortis set are realized as a sequence of /h/ followed by a single segment drawn from the set of lenis consonants: /p t k tʃ s ʃ/. Algonquin Ojibwe is reported as distinguishing fortis and lenis consonants on the basis of voicing, with fortis being voiceless and lenis being voiced. In other dialects fortis consonants are realized as having greater duration than the corresponding lenis consonant, invariably voiceless, 'vigorously articulated,' and aspirated in certain environments. In some practical orthographies such as the widely used Double Vowel system, fortis consonants are written with voiceless symbols: *p, t, k, ch, s, sh*.

Lenis consonants have normal duration; are typically voiced intervocalically, although they may be devoiced at the end or beginning of a word; are less vigorously articulated than fortis consonants; and are invariably unaspirated. In the Double Vowel practical orthography, lenis consonants are written with voiced symbols: *b, d, g, j, z, zh*.

All dialects of Ojibwe have two nasal consonants /m/ and /n/; one labialized velar approximant /w/; one palatal approximant /j/; and one of glottal stop /ʔ/ or /h/.

All dialects of Ojibwe have seven oral vowels. Vowel length is phonologically contrastive, hence phonemic. Although the long and short vowels are phonetically distinguished by vowel quality, recognition of vowel length in phonological representations is required, as the distinction between long and short vowels is essential for the operation of the metrical rule of vowel syncope that characterizes the Ottawa and Eastern Ojibwe dialects, as well as for the rules that determine word stress. There are three short vowels, /i a o/; and three corresponding long vowels, /iː aː oː/, in addition to a fourth long vowel /eː/, which lacks a corresponding short vowel. The short vowel /i/ typically has phonetic values centring on [ɪ]; /a/ typically has values centring on [ə]~[ʌ]; and /o/ typically has values centring on [o]~[ʊ]. Long /oː/ is pronounced [uː] for many speakers, and /eː/ is for many [ɛː].

Ojibwe has nasal vowels; some arise predictably by rule in all analyses, and other long nasal vowels are of uncertain phonological status. The latter have been analysed both as underlying phonemes, and also as predictable, that is derived by the operation of phonological rules from sequences of a long vowel followed by /n/ and another segment, typically /j/.

Placement of word stress is determined by metrical rules that define a characteristic iambic metrical Foot, in which a Weak syllable is followed by a Strong syllable. A Foot consists of a minimum of one syllable, and a maximum of two syllables, with each Foot containing a maximum of one Strong syllable. The structure of the metrical Foot defines the domain for relative prominence, in which a Strong syllable is assigned stress because it is more prominent than the weak member of the Foot. Typically, the Strong syllable in the antepenultimate Foot is assigned the primary stress. Strong syllables that do not receive main stress are assigned at least secondary stress. In some dialects, metrically Weak (unstressed) vowels at the beginning of a word are frequently lost; in the Ottawa and Eastern Ojibwe dialects all metrically Weak vowels are deleted.

Grammar

Main article: Ojibwe grammar

The general grammatical characteristics of Ojibwe are shared across its dialects. The Ojibwe language is polysynthetic, exhibits characteristics of synthesis and a high morpheme-to-word ratio. Ojibwe is a head-marking language in which inflectional morphology on nouns and particularly verbs carries significant amounts of grammatical information.

Word classes include nouns, verbs, grammatical particles, pronouns, preverbs, and prenouns. Preferred word orders in a simple transitive sentence are verb-initial, such as V(erb) O(bject) S(ubject) and VSO. While verb-final orders are dispreferred, all logically possible orders are attested.

Complex inflectional and derivational morphology play a central role in Ojibwe grammar. Noun inflection and particularly verb inflection indicate a wide variety of grammatical information, realized through the use of prefixes and suffixes added to word stems. Grammatical characteristics include the following:

1. gender, divided into animate and inanimate categories
2. extensive head-marking on verbs of inflectional information concerning person
3. number
4. tense
5. modality
6. evidentiality
7. negation
8. a distinction between obviative and proximate third-person, marked on both verbs and nouns.

There is a distinction between two different types of third person, the *proximate* (the third person deemed more important or in-focus) and the *obviative* (the third person deemed less important or out-of-focus). Nouns can be singular or plural, and one of two genders, animate or inanimate. Separate personal pronouns exist, but are usually used for emphasis; they distinguish inclusive and exclusive first person plurals.

Verbs constitute the most complex word class. Verbs are inflected for one of three *orders* (*indicative*, the default; *conjunct*, used for participles and in subordinate clauses; and *imperative*, used with commands), as negative or affirmative, and for the person, number, animacy, and proximate/obviative status of both the subject and object, as well as for several different *modes* (including the *dubitative* and *preterit*) and tenses.

Vocabulary

Loanwords and neologisms

Although it does contain a few loans from English (e.g. *gaapii*, "coffee,") and French (e.g. *mooshwe*, "handkerchief" (from *mouchoir*), *ni-tii*, "tea" (from *le thé*, "the tea")), in general, the Ojibwe language is notable for its relative lack of borrowing from other languages. Instead, speakers far prefer to create words for new concepts from existing vocabulary. For example in Minnesota *Ojibwemowin*, "airplane" is *bemisemagak*, literally "thing that flies" (from *bimisemagad*, "to fly"), and "battery" is *ishkode-makakoons*, literally "little fire-box" (from *ishkode*, "fire," and *makak*, "box"). Even "coffee" is called *makade-mashkikiwaaboo* ("black liquid-medicine") by many speakers, rather than *gaapii*. These new words vary from region to region, and occasionally from community to community. For example, in Northwest Ontario *Ojibwemowin*, "airplane" is *ombaasijigan*, literally "device that gets uplifted by the wind" (from *ombaasin*, "to be uplifted by the wind") oppose to the Minnesota's *bemisemagak*.

Dialect variation

Like any language dialects spanning vast regions, some words that may have had identical meaning at one time have evolved to have different meanings today. For example, *zhooniyaans* (literally "small[-amount of] money" and used to refer to coins) specifically means "dime" (10-cent piece) in the United States, but a "quarter" (25-cent piece) in Canada, or *desabiwin* (literally "thing to sit upon") means "couch" or "chair" in Canada, but is used to specifically mean a "saddle" in the United States.

Cases like "battery" and "coffee" also demonstrate the often great difference between the literal meanings of the individual morphemes in a word, and the overall meaning of the entire word.

Sample vocabulary

Below are some examples of common Ojibwe words.

Short List of VAIs:
onjibaa = he/she comes
izhaa = he/she goes
maajaa = he/she departs
pikade = he/she is hungry
mino'endamo = he/she is glad
zhaaganaashimo = he/she speaks English
biindige = he/she comes in
ojibwemo = he/she speaks Ojibwe
boogidi = he/she flatulates
boogide = he/she has flatulence
aadizooke = he/she tells a story
wiisini = he/she is eating
minikwe = he/she drinks
bimose = he/she walks
bangishino = he/she falls
digoshino = he/she is arriving
giiwe = he/she goes home
jiibaakwe = he/she cooks
zagaswe = he/she smokes
nibaa = he/she sleeps
giigoonyike = he/she is fishing (lit. he/she makes fish)
gashkendamo = he/she is sad
bimaadizi = he/she lives
gaasikanaabaagawe = he/she is thirsty

Short List of Nouns:
naboob = soup
ikwe = woman
inini = man
ikwezens = girl
gwiiwizens = boy
mitigo = tree
asemaa = tobacco
opwaagan = pipe
mandaamin = corn
manoomin = wild rice
miskwi = blood
doodooshaaboo = milk
doodoosh = breast
doodooshaaboo-bimide = butter
omanoominiig = Menomonee peoples
giigoonh = fish
miskwimin = raspberry
gekek = hawk
gookookoo'oo = owl
migizi = bald eagle
giniw = golden eagle
bemaadizid = person
bemaadizijig = people
makizin = mocassin, shoe
wiigiwaam = wigwam, house

Writing system

Main article: Ojibwe writing systems

There is no standard writing system used for all Ojibwe dialects. Local writing systems have been developed by adapting the Roman alphabet, usually from English or French writing systems. A syllabic writing system not related to English or French writing is used by some Ojibwe speakers in northern Ontario and Manitoba. The Great Lakes Algonquian syllabary is based upon the French alphabet, with letters organized into syllables. It was primarily used by speakers of Fox, Potawatomi, and Winnebago, but there is indirect evidence of use by speakers of Southwestern Ojibwe.

A widely used Roman character-based writing system is the Double Vowel system devised by Charles Fiero. Although there is no standard orthography, the Double Vowel system is used by many Ojibwe language teachers because of its ease of use. A wide range of materials have been published in this system, including a grammar, dictionaries, collections of texts, and pedagogical grammars. In northern Ontario and Manitoba, Ojibwe is most commonly written using the Cree syllabary, a syllabary originally developed by Methodist missionary James Evans around 1840 in order to write Cree. The syllabic system is based in part on Evans' knowledge of Pitman shorthand and his prior experience developing a distinctive alphabetic writing system for Ojibwe in southern Ontario.

Double Vowel System

The Double Vowel System uses three short vowels, four long vowels, and eighteen consonants, represented with the following Roman letters:

a aa b ch d e g ' h i ii j k m n o oo p s sh t w y z zh

Dialects typically either have /h/ or /ʔ/ (the orthographic <'> in most versions) but rarely both. This system is called "Double Vowel" because the long vowel correspondences to the short vowels <a>, <i> and <o> are written with a doubled value. In this system, the nasal "ny" as a final element is instead written as "nh." The allowable consonant clusters are <mb>, <nd>, <ng>, <n'>, <nj>, <nz>, <ns>, <nzh>, <sk>, <shp>, <sht> and <shk>.

Sample text and analysis

The sample text, from the Southwestern Ojibwe dialect, is taken, with permission, from the first four lines of Niizh Ikwewag [9], a story originally told by Earl Nyholm, on Professor Brian Donovan of Bemidji State University's webpage.

Text

1. *Aabiding gii-ayaawag niizh ikwewag: mindimooyenh, odaanisan bezhig.*
2. *Iwidi Chi-achaabaaning akeyaa gii-onjibaawag.*
3. *Inashke naa mewinzha gii-aawan, mii eta go imaa sa wiigiwaaming gaa-taawaad igo.*
4. *Mii dash iwapii, aabiding igo gii-awi-bagida'waawaad, giigoonyan wii-amwaawaad.*

Translation

1. Once there were two women: an old lady, and one of her daughters.
2. They were from over there towards Inger.
3. See now, it was long ago; they just lived there in a wigwam.
4. And at that time, once they went net-fishing; they intended to eat fish.

Gloss

Aabiding	gii-ayaawag			niizh	ikwewag:		mindimooyenh,	odaanisan			bezhig.
aabiding	gii-	ayaa	-wag	niizh	ikwe	-wag	mindimooyenh,	o-	daanis	-an	bezhig.
once	PAST-	be in a certain place	-3PL	two	woman	-3PL	old woman,	3SG.POSS-	daughter	-OBV	one.
Once	*they were in a certain place*			*two*	*women:*		*old woman,*	*her daughter*			*one.*

Iwidi	Chi-achaabaaning			akeyaa	gii-onjibaawag.		
iwidi	chi-	achaabaan	-ing	akeyaa	gii-	onjibaa	-wag.
over there	big-	bowstring	-LOC	that way	PAST-	come from	-3PL.
Over there	*by Inger* *(lit: by Big-Bowstring [River])*			*that way*	*they came from there.*		

Inashke	naa	mewinzha	gii-aawan,		mii eta go		imaa	sa	wiigiwaaming		gaa-taawaad			igo.
inashke	naa	mewinzha	gii-	aawan	mii eta	go	imaa	sa	wiigiwaam	-ing	gaa-	daa	-waad	igo.
look	now	long ago	PAST-	be	so only	EMPH	there	EMPH	wigwam	-LOC	PAST.CONJ-	live	-3PL.CONJ	EMPH.
Look	*now*	*long ago*	*it was,*		*only*		*there*	*so*	*in a wigwam*		*that they lived*			*just then.*

Mii dash		iwapii,		aabiding	igo	gii-awi-bagida'waawaad,				giigoonyan		wii-amwaawaad.		
mii	dash	iw-	-apii	aabiding	igo	gii-	awi-	bagida'waa	-waad,	giigoonh	-yan	wii-	amw	-aawaad.
it is that	CONTR	that-	-then	once	EMPH	PAST-	go and-	fish with a net	-3PL.CONJ	fish	-OBV	DESD-	eat	-3PL/OBV.CONJ
And then		*then,*		*once*	*just then*	*that they went and fished with a net*				*those fish*		*that they are going to eat those*		

Abbreviations:

3	third person
SG	singular
PL	plural
POSS	possessive
OBV	obviative
LOC	locative
EMPH	emphatic particle
CONJ	conjunct order
CONTR	contrastive particle
DESD	desiderative

Well-known speakers of Anishinaabemowin

- The 19th century missionary bishop Frederic Baraga, who wrote *A theoretical and practical grammar of the Otchipwe language* [10]
- Jim Clark (elder, narrator)
- George Copway (chief, missionary, writer, cultural ambassador)
- Basil H. Johnston (educator, curator, essayist, cultural ambassador)
- Peter Jones (missionary, reverend, chief)
- Maude Kegg (narrator, artist, cultural ambassador)
- Caroline Helen Roy Fuhst (educator, writer, singer)
- Howard Kimewon (educator, author)
- Patricia Ningewance Nadeau (educator, author, publisher)
- Margaret Noori (educator, writer)
- Jim Northrup (writer)
- Anton Treuer (educator, writer)

See also

- Canadian Aboriginal syllabics
- Algonquian languages
- List of languages
- Ojibwa
- Anishinaabe
- Anishinaabe language dialects
- Ojibwe phonology

- Ojibwe grammar
- Ojibwe writing systems

References

- Bakker, Peter. 1991. "The Ojibwa element in Michif." W. Cowan, ed., *Papers of the twenty-second Algonquian conference,* 11-20. Ottawa: Carleton University. ISSN 0031-5671 [11]
- Bakker, Peter. 1996. *A language of our own: The genesis of Michif, the mixed Cree-French language of the Canadian Métis.* New York: Oxford University Press. ISBN 0-19-509711-4
- Bakker, Peter and Anthony Grant. 1996. "Interethnic communication in Canada, Alaska and adjacent areas." Stephen A. Wurm, Peter Muhlhausler, Darrell T. Tyron, eds., *Atlas of Languages of Intercultural Communication in the Pacific, Asia, and the Americas,* 1107-1170. Berlin: Mouton de Gruyter. ISBN 978-3110134179
- Bloomfield, Leonard. 1958. *Eastern Ojibwa: Grammatical sketch, texts and word list.* Ann Arbor: University of Michigan Press.
- Bloomfield, Leonard. 1962. *The Menomini language.* New Haven: Yale University Press.
- [Dawes, Charles E.] 1982. *Dictionary English-Ottawa Ottawa-English.* No publisher given.
- Canada. Statistics Canada 2006 [12] Retrieved on March 31, 2009.
- Feest, Johanna, and Christian Feest. 1978. "Ottawa." Bruce Trigger, ed., *The Handbook of North American Indians, Volume 15. Northeast,* 772-786. Washington, D.C.: The Smithsonian Institution.
- Goddard, Ives. 1978. "Central Algonquian Languages." Bruce Trigger, ed., *Handbook of North American Indians, Volume 15, Northeast,* 583-587. Washington: Smithsonian Institution.
- Goddard, Ives. 1979. "Comparative Algonquian." Lyle Campbell and Marianne Mithun, eds, *The languages of Native America,* 70-132. Austin: University of Texas Press.
- Goddard, Ives. 1996. "Introduction." Ives Goddard, ed., *The Handbook of North American Indians, Volume 17. Languages,* 1-16. Washington, D.C.: The Smithsonian Institution.
- Gordon Jr., Raymond. 2005. *Ethnologue: Languages of the World, 15th edition.* Ethnologue entry for Ojibwe [13]. Retrieved March 31, 2009. Dallas: SIL International. ISBN 978-1-55671-159-6
- Kegg, Maude. 1991. Edited and transcribed by John D. Nichols. *Portage Lake: Memories of an Ojibwe Childhood.* Edmonton: University of Alberta Press. ISBN 081662-4151
- Laverdure, Patline and Ida Rose Allard. 1983. *The Michif dictionary: Turtle Mountain Chippewa Cree.* Winnipeg, MB: Pemmican Publications. ISBN 0919143350
- Nichols, John. 1980. *Ojibwe morphology.* PhD dissertation, Harvard University.
- Nichols, John. 1995. "The Ojibwe verb in "Broken Oghibbeway." *Amsterdam Creole Studies* 12: 1-18.
- Nichols, John. 1996. "The Cree syllabary." Peter Daniels and William Bright, eds. *The world's writing systems,* 599-611. New York: Oxford University Press. ISBN 0-19-507993-0

- Nichols, John D. and Leonard Bloomfield, eds. 1991. *The dog's children. Anishinaabe texts told by Angeline Williams.* Winnipeg: Publications of the Algonquian Text Society, University of Manitoba. ISBN 0-88755-148-3
- Nichols, John and Earl Nyholm. 1995. *A concise dictionary of Minnesota Ojibwe.* St. Paul: University of Minnesota Press. ISBN 0-8166-2427-5
- Ningewance, Patricia. 1993. *Survival Ojibwe.* Winnipeg: Mazinaate Press. ISBN 0-9697826-0-8
- Ningewance, Patricia. 1999. *Naasaab izhi-anishinaabebii'igeng: Conference report. A conference to find a common Anishinaabemowin writing system.* Toronto: Queen's Printer for Ontario. ISBN 0-7778-8695-2
- Ningewance, Patricia. 2004. *Talking Gookom's language: Learning Ojibwe.* Lac Seul, ON: Mazinaate Press. ISBN 0-969782-3-2
- Piggott, Glyne L. 1980. *Aspects of Odawa morphophonemics.* New York: Garland. (Published version of PhD dissertation, University of Toronto, 1974) ISBN 0-8240-4557-2
- Rhodes, Richard. 1976. "A preliminary report on the dialects of Eastern Ojibwa-Odawa." W. Cowan, ed., *Papers of the seventh Algonquian conference,* 129-156. Ottawa: Carleton University.
- Rhodes, Richard. 1982. "Algonquian trade languages." William Cowan, ed., *Papers of the thirteenth Algonquian conference,* 1-10. Ottawa: Carleton University. ISBN 0-7709-0123-9
- Rhodes, Richard A. 1985. *Eastern Ojibwa-Chippewa-Ottawa Dictionary.* Berlin: Mouton de Gruyter. ISBN 3-11-013749-6
- Rhodes, Richard and Evelyn Todd. 1981. "Subarctic Algonquian languages." June Helm, ed., *The Handbook of North American Indians, Volume 6. Subarctic,* 52-66. Washington, D.C.: The Smithsonian Institution.
- Smith, Huron H. 1932. "Ethnobotany of the Ojibwe Indians." *Bulletin of the Public Museum of Milwaukee* 4:327-525.
- Todd, Evelyn. 1970. *A grammar of the Ojibwa language: The Severn dialect.* PhD dissertation, University of North Carolina, Chapel Hill.
- U.S. Census Bureau, 2000 Census of Population and Housing. *Characteristics of American Indians and Alaska Natives by Tribe and Language: 2000* [14] Retrieved on March 31, 2009.
- Valentine, J. Randolph. 1994. *Ojibwe dialect relationships.* PhD dissertation, University of Texas, Austin.
- Valentine, J. Randolph. 1998. *Weshki-bimaadzijig ji-noondmowaad. 'That the young might hear': The stories of Andrew Medler as recorded by Leonard Bloomfield.* London, ON: The Centre for Teaching and Research of Canadian Native Languages, University of Western Ontario. ISBN 0-7714-2091-9
- Valentine, J. Randolph. 2001. *Nishnaabemwin Reference Grammar.* Toronto: University of Toronto Press. ISBN 0-8020-4870-6
- Vollom, Judith L. and Thomas M. Vollom. 1994. *Ojibwemowin. Series 1.* Second Edition. Ramsey, Minnesota: Ojibwe Language Publishing.

- Walker, Willard. 1996. "Native writing systems." Ives Goddard, ed., *The Handbook of North American Indians, Volume 17. Languages,* 158-184. Washington, D.C.: The Smithsonian Institution. ISBN 0-16-048774-9

Further reading

- Beardy, Tom. *Introductory Ojibwe in Severn dialect. Parts one and two.* Thunder Bay, Ontario: Native Language Instructors' program, Lakehead University, 1996. ISBN 0886630185
- Cappel, Constance, editor, "Odawa Language and legends: Andrew J. Blackbird and Raymond Kiogima," Philadelphia: Xlibris, 2006. ISBN 9781599269207
- Hinton, Leanne and Kenneth Hale. 2001. *The Green Book of Language Revitalization in Practice.* Academic Press. ISBN 0123493534
- McGregor, Ernest. 1987. *Algonquin lexicon.* Maniwaki, QC: River Desert Education Authority.
- Mitchell, Mary. 1988. Eds. J. Randolph Valentine and Lisa Valentine. *Introductory Ojibwe (Severn dialect), Part one.* Thunder Bay: Native Language Office, Lakehead University.
- Mithun, Marianne. 1999. *The Languages of Native North America.* Cambridge: University Press. ISBN 0521232287
- Moose, Lawrence L. et al., *Aaniin Ekidong: Ojibwe Vocabulary Project*Aaniin Ekidong: Ojibwe Vocabulary Project [15]. St. Paul: Minnesota Humanities Center, 2009.
- Ningewance, Patricia. 1990. *Anishinaabemodaa: Becoming a successful Ojibwe eavesdropper.* Winnipeg: Manitoba Association for Native Languages. ISBN 189463201X
- Northrup, Jim, Marcie R. Rendon, and Linda LeGarde Grover. *Nitaawichige = "to Do Something Skillfully" : Selected Poetry and Prose by Four Anishinaabe Writers.* Duluth, MN: Poetry Harbor, 2002. ISBN 1886895287
- Snache, Irene. 2005. *Ojibwe language dictionary.*Rama, ON: Mnjikaning Kendaaswin Publishers. ISBN 189463201X
- Sugarhead, Cecilia. 1996. ᖱᖱᖱᖱ / *Ninoontaan / I can hear it: Ojibwe stories from Lansdowne House written by Cecilia Sugarhead.* Edited, translated and with a glossary by John O'Meara. Winnipeg: Algonquian and Iroquoian Linguistics. ISBN 0921064144
- Toulouse, Isadore. *Kidwenan An Ojibwe Language Book.* Munsee-Delaware Nation, ON: Anishinaabe Kendaaswin Pub, 1995. ISBN 1896027164
- Treuer, Anton. *Living our language: Ojibwe tales & oral histories* [16]. St. Paul, MN: Minnesota Historical Society Press, 2001. ISBN 0873514041
- Treuer, Anton. *Ojibwe in Minnesota*Ojibwe in Minnesota [17]. St. Paul: Minnesota Historical Society Press, 2010.
- Vizenor, Gerald Robert. *Summer in the Spring Anishinaabe Lyric Poems and Stories.* American Indian literature and critical studies series, v. 6. Norman: University of Oklahoma Press, 1993. ISBN 0806125187

- Williams, Shirley I. 2002. *Gdi-nweninaa: Our sound, our voice.* Peterborough, ON: Neganigwane. ISBN 0973144211

External links

- A theoretical and practical grammar of the Otchipwe language [10] by Frederic Baraga
- *Noongwa e-Anishinaabemjig*: People Who Speak Anishinaabemowin Today [18] — hosted at the University of Michigan
- Ojibwe Language Society [19]
- Ojibwe Language Group [20]
- Language Museum report for Ojibwe [21]
- Aboriginal Languages of Canada [22] — With data on speaker populations
- Language Geek Page on Ojibwe [23] — Syllabary fonts and keyboard emulators are also available from this site.
- Ojibwe Toponyms [24]
- *Niizh Ikwewag* [9] — A short story in Ojibwe, originally told by Earl Nyholm, emeritus professor of Ojibwe at Bemidji State University.
- Ethnologue report for Ojibwe [13]
- Native Languages: A Support Document for the Teaching of Language Patterns, Ojibwe and Cree [25]
- Native Languages page for Ojibwe [26]
- Letter Men: Brothers Fight for Ojibwe Language [27], a story broadcast on Fresh Air, a National Public Radio broadcast show.
- Language and Meaning — An Ojibwe Story [28], a story broadcast on Speaking of Faith, a National Public Radio broadcast show.
- *Bemaadizing:* An Interdisciplinary Journal of Indigenous Life [29] (An online journal)
- Comprehensive list of learning resources for Ojibwe [30] prepared for the SSILA by Dr. Rand Valentine

Grammar and Lessons

- Comparative Ojibwe Swadesh vocabulary list of basic words [31] (from Wiktionary's Swadesh list appendix [32])
- Rand Valentine's introduction to Ojibwe [33]
- Grammar, lessons, and dictionaries [34] — Ojibwe site by "*Weshki-ayaad*"
- *Gikendandaa Ojibwemowin* [35] — Ojibwe lesson site by James Starkey (*Mindjime*)
- Native Languages: A Support Document for the Teaching of Language Patters [25] — basic language patterns for Ojibwe (Manitoulin Ojibwe/Ottawa "CO" and Lac Seul Ojibwe "WO") and Cree (Swampy Cree "SC").

- Baraga, Frederic (Bishop) (1878). *A Theoretical and Practical Grammar of the Otchipwe Language for the Use of Missionaries and Other Persons Living Among the Indians* [10].

Dictionaries and Wordlists

- *Aaniin Ekidong...* (How Do You Say...): Ojibwe Vocabulary Project [15] — Math and science terms for the Southwestern (Wisconsin, Leech Lake and Red Lake) and Minnesota Border Chippewa dialect of the Ojibwe language.
- Our Languages: Nakawē [36] (Saskatchewan Indian Cultural Centre)
- *Anishinaabe-Ikidowinan* (Ojibwe) Dictionary [37] — Courtesy of the Kwayaciiwin Education Resource Centre. Covers Berens River and English River dialects of Northwestern Ojibwe
- Freelang Ojibwe Dictionary [38] — Freeware off-line dictionary, updated with additional entries every 6–10 weeks.
- Kees van Kolmeschate: My Ojibwe Documents [39] — Assorted digital Ojibwe-related documents, including the electronic version of the 1878 Baraga Dictionary.
- Baraga, Frederic (Bishop). *Dictionary of the Otchipwe Language, Explained in English.*
  - Part I: English-Otchipwe and Part II: Otchipwe-English in the 1853 edition [40] at Wisconsin Historical Society
  - Part I: English-Otchipwe in the 1878 edition [41] and Part II: Otchipwe-English in the 1880 edition [42] courtesy of Google Books

Potawatomi language

Potawatomi	
Neshnabémwen	
Spoken in	United States, Canada
Region	Michigan, Indiana, Wisconsin, Kansas, and southern Ontario
Total speakers	50
Language family	Algic • Algonquian • Potawatomi
Language codes	
ISO 639-1	*None*
ISO 639-2	`alg`
ISO 639-3	`pot` [1]
Linguasphere	

Potawatomi (also spelled **Pottawatomie**; in Potawatomi **Bodéwadmimwen** or **Bodéwadmi Zheshmowen** or **Neshnabémwen**) is a Central Algonquian language and is spoken around the Great Lakes in Michigan and Wisconsin, as well as in Kansas in the United States, and in southern Ontario in Canada, by fewer than 10 Potawatomi people, all elderly. There is currently an effort underway to revive the language.

Classification

Potawatomi is a member of the Algonquian language family (itself a member of the larger Algic stock). It is usually classified as a Central Algonquian Language, along with languages such as Ojibwe, Cree, Menominee, Miami-Illinois, Shawnee and Fox but the label "Central Algonquian" signifies a geographic grouping, rather than that the group of languages descended from a common ancestor language within the Algonquian family. Of these languages, Potawatomi is most similar to Ojibwe, however it also has borrowed a considerable amount of vocabulary from Sauk.

Writing systems

Current writing system

Though no standard orthography has been agreed upon by the Potawatomi communities, the system most commonly used is the "Pedagogical System" developed by the Wisconsin Native American Languages Program. As the name suggests, this writing system was designed to be used in language teaching. The system is alphabetic (based on the Roman Alphabet), and is phonemic, with each letter or digraph representing a contrastive sound. The letters used are: a b ch d e é g h ' i j k m n o p s sh t w y z zh.

Traditional system

The "Traditional System" used in writing Potawatomi is an alphabetic system. Letters are written in syllable groups. Potawatomi, Ottawa, Sac, Fox and Winnebago communities all used this form of syllabic writing. The System was derived from the Roman Alphabet, thus it resembles hand-written Roman text. However, unlike the Unified Canadian Aboriginal Syllabics or the Cherokee alphabet, this writing system has not yet been incorporated into the Unicode standards.

Each Potawatomi Syllabic block in the Traditional System consists of at least two of the 17 alphabetic letters: 13 consonants and 4 vowels. Of the 13 phonemic consonantal letters, the <h> written with [A] was considered optional.

Consonants		Consonants		Consonants		Vowels	
Traditional System	Pedagogical System	Traditional System	Pedagogical System	Traditional System	Pedagogical System	Traditional System	Pedagogical System
l	b/p	*(KA)*	(k)	*q*	gw/kw	*a*	a
(lA)	(p)	*s*	z/s	*(qA)*	(kw)	*e*	e
t	d/t	*(sA)*	s	*g*	g of "-ng"	*e*	é
(tA)	(t)	*sH*	zh/sh	*w*	w	*i*	i
tt	j/ch	*(sHA)*	(sh)	*y*	y	*o*	o
(ttA)	(ch)	*m*	m	<none>	'/h		
K	g/k	*n*	n	*(A)*	(h)		

Sounds

In this article, the phonology of the Northern dialect is described, which differs somewhat from that of the Southern dialect spoken in Kansas.

There are five vowel phonemes (plus four diphthongs) and nineteen consonant phonemes.

<é>, which is often written as <e'>, represents an open-mid front unrounded vowel, IPA: [ɛ]. <e> represents the schwa, /ə/, which has several allophonic variants. Before /n/, it becomes [ɪ], and Before /k/, /g/, and /ʔ/, and word-finally, it is [ʌ]. <o> is pronounced /u/ in Michigan, and /o/ elsewhere; when it is in a closed syllable, it is pronounced [ʊ]. There are also four diphthongs, /ɛj ɛw əj əw/, spelled <éy éw ey ew>. Phonemic /əj əw/ are realized as [ɪj ʌw].

The obstruents, as in many Algonquian languages, do not have a voicing distinction per se, but rather what is better termed a "strong"/"weak" distinction. "Strong" consonants, written as voiceless (<p t k kw>), are always voiceless, are often aspirated, and are longer in duration than the "weak" consonants, which are written as voiced (<b d g gw>) and are often voiced and are never aspirated. Nasals before another consonant become syllabic. /t/, /d/, and /n/ are dental: [t̪ d̪ n̪].

Vowels

	Front	Central	Back
Close	i		
Close-mid			o
Mid		e	
Open-mid	é		
Open		a	

Consonants

	Bilabial	Dental	Palatal	Velar	Labio-velar	Glottal
Plosive	p b	t d		k g	kw gw	ʼ
Affricate			ch j			
Fricative		s z	sh zh			h
Nasal	m	n				
Semivowel			y		w	

Grammar

Potawatomi has six parts of speech, which are: noun, verb, pronoun, prenoun, preverb, and particle.

Pronouns

There are two main types of pronoun, personal pronouns and demonstrative pronouns. As nouns and verbs use inflection to describe anaphoric reference the main use of the free pronouns is for emphasis.

Personal pronouns

Potawatomi	Gloss
nin	I
gin	you
win	he, she
ninan	we (exclusive)
ginan	we (inclusive)
ginwa	you (plural)
winwa	they

Correspondence to the Ojibwe language

Due to the relatively recent diversion from the Ojibwe language, the Potawatomi language still exhibits strong correspondences to the Ojibwe language, and more specifically with the *Odaawaa* (Ottawa) dialect.

Fiero Double Vowel System	Rhodes Double Vowel System	Potawatomi System	IPA Value
a (unstressed)	<none>	<none>	<none>
a (stressed)	a (stressed)	e	ə
aa	aa	a	a~ʌ
b	b	b	b
ch	ch	ch	tʃ
d	d	d	d
e (unstressed)	e (unstressed)	e	ə
e (stressed)	e (stressed)	é	ɛ

g	g	g	g
h	h	h	h
'	h	'	ʔ
i (unstressed)	<none>	<none>	<none>
i (stressed)	i (stressed)	e	ə
ii	ii	i	ɪ
j	j	j	dʒ
k	k	k/ch	k/tʃ
m	m	m	m
mb	mb	mb	mb
(not from PA *n) n/<none>	n/<none>	n/y	n/j
(from PA *n) n	n	n	n
nd	nd	nd	nd
ng	ng	ng	ŋg
nj	nj	nj	ndʒ
ns	ns	s	s
nz	nz	z	z
ny/-nh	ny/-nh	<none>	<none>
nzh	nzh	zh	ʒ
o (unstressed)	<none>/w/o (unstressed)	<none>/w/o/e	<none>/w/o~[ʊ]/ə
o (stressed)	o (stressed)	o	o~[ʊ]
oo	oo	o	o
p	p	p	p
s	s	s	s
sh	sh	sh	ʃ
shk	shk	shk	ʃk
shp	shp	shp	ʃp
sht	sht	sht	ʃt
sk	sk	sk	sk
t	t	t	t

w	w/<none>	w/<none>	w/<none>
wa (unstressed)	wa (unstressed)/o	w/o	w/o~[ʊ]
waa (unstressed)	waa (unstressed)/oo	wa/o	wa/o~[ʊ]
wi (unstressed)	wi (unstressed)/o	w/o	w/o~[ʊ]
y	y	y (initial glide)	j
<none>	<none>	y (medial glide)	j
z	z	z	z
zh	zh	zh	ʒ

Further reading

- Gailland, Maurice. *English-Potawatomi Dictionary*. 1840.
- Hockett, Charles Francis. *The Potawatomi Language A Descriptive Grammar*. Ann Arbor, Mich: University Microfilms International, 1987.
- Hockett, Charles Francis. *Potawatomi Syntax*. 1939.
- Quimby, George Irving. *Some Notes on Kinship and Kinship Terminology Among the Potawatomi of the Huron*. S.l: s.n, 1940.
- Wisconsin Native American Languages Project, and John Nichols. *Potawatomi Traditional Writing*. Milwaukee Wis: Great Lakes Inter-Tribal Council, 1975.

External links

- Potawatomi Language Vocabulary, Audio and Video, Interactive Language Games, Online Courses [2]
- Ethnologue report for Potawatomi [3]
- The Neshnabe Institute for Cultural Studies - Dedicated to Potawatomi Language Revitalization [4]
- Prairie Band Potawatomi Language Project [5] Smokey McKinney, 1997

Geography

West Alaska Lake

West Alaska Lake	
Location	Kewaunee County, Wisconsin
Coordinates	44°32′26″N 87°30′19″W
Basin countries	United States
Average depth	15 ft (4.6 m)
Max. depth	41 ft (12 m)
Surface elevation	696 ft (212 m)
Settlements	Alaska, Wisconsin

West Alaska Lake, is a small lake in Central Kewaunee County, Wisconsin. The lake is home to bluegill, brook trout, largemouth bass and rainbow trout. The lake shares the area with its larger neighbor, East Alaska Lake because of that the lake is a popular fishing destination.

References

- U.S. Geological Survey Geographic Names Information System: West Alaska Lake [1]
- General lake information [2]

Kettle Moraine

Kettle Moraine is a large moraine in the state of Wisconsin stretching from Walworth County in the south to Kewaunee County in the north. It has also been referred to as the **Kettle Range** and, in geological texts, as the **Kettle Interlobate Moraine**.

The moraine was created when the Green Bay Lobe of the glacier, on the west, collided with the Lake Michigan Lobe of the glacier, on the east, depositing sediment. The western glacier formed the Bay of Green Bay, Lake Winnebago and the Horicon Marsh while the eastern one formed Lake Michigan. The major part of the Kettle Moraine area is considered interlobate moraine, though other types of moraine features, and other glacial features are common.

The moraine is dotted with kettles caused by buried glacial ice that subsequently melted. This process left depressions ranging from small ponds to large lakes and enclosed valleys. Elkhart Lake, Geneva Lake, Big Cedar Lake are among the larger kettles now filled by lakes.

Parts of the area have been protected in the Kettle Moraine State Forest.

External links

- Summary of the geological history of Kettle Moraine [1] from the Wisconsin Department of Natural Resources
- "Northern Kettle Interlobate Moraine" [2], from *Geology of Ice Age National Scientific Reserve of Wisconsin* [3] by Robert F. Black

Krohns Lake

Krohns Lake	
Location	Kewaunee County, Wisconsin
Coordinates	44°35′01″N 87°29′19″W
Primary inflows	*springs*
Basin countries	United States
Surface area	21 acres (8.5 ha)
Average depth	21 ft (6.4 m)
Max. depth	38 ft (12 m)
Surface elevation	665 ft (203 m)

Krohns Lake, is a spring fed lake Southwest of Algoma, Wisconsin in Kewaunee County. The lake is part of the Tri-Lakes Association who is in charge of this lake, East Alaska Lake, and West Alaska Lake.

Fish species

- Bluegill
- Brook trout
- Brown trout
- Largemouth bass
- Rainbow trout

References

- U.S. Geological Survey Geographic Names Information System: Krohns Lake [1]
- General Lake information [2]
- Lake Association information [3]

Green Bay (Lake Michigan)

Green Bay is an arm of Lake Michigan, located along the south coast of Michigan's Upper Peninsula and the east coast of Wisconsin. It is separated from the rest of the lake by the Door Peninsula in Wisconsin, the Garden Peninsula in Michigan, and the chain of islands between them, all formed by the Niagara Escarpment. Green Bay is some 120 miles (193 km) long, with a width ranging from about 10 miles (16 km) to 20 mi (32 km). It is 1626 square miles (4210 km^2) in area.

A Tall ship sailing into the mouth of the Fox River

At the southern end of the bay is the city of Green Bay, Wisconsin, where the Fox River enters the bay. The Leo Frigo Memorial Bridge (formerly known as the Tower Drive bridge) spans the point where the bay ends and the Fox River begins. Locally, the bay is often called the **Bay of Green Bay** to distinguish the bay from the city. The bay is navigable by large ships.

The bay was named *Baie des Puants* (literally, "Bay of the Stinkers") during the French regime as attested by many French maps of the 17th and 18th centuries. The stench apparently came from algae in the stagnant water of the bay. According to George R. Stewart, the French received the name from their Indian guides, who called the Indians living near Green Bay by a derogatory word meaning "Stinkers", thus the bay was the "Bay of the Stinkers" (Stewart 1967:88).

The bay is located in parts of five counties in Wisconsin (Brown, Door, Kewaunee, Marinette, Oconto), and two in Michigan (Delta, Menominee).

References
- Stewart, George R. (1967) Names on the Land. Boston: Houghton Mifflin Company.

Notes
Geographical coordinates: 44°55′17″N 087°32′34″W

East Alaska Lake

East Alaska Lake	
Location	Kewaunee County, Wisconsin
Coordinates	44°32′42″N 87°30′03″W
Basin countries	United States
Surface area	53 acres (21 ha)
Average depth	17 ft (5.2 m)
Max. depth	50 ft (15 m)
Surface elevation	696 ft (212 m)
Settlements	Alaska, Wisconsin

East Alaska Lake is a lake in central Kewaunee County, Wisconsin, it is the biggest inland lake in the county. The lake is located on a golf course. Fish in the lake include Bluegill, Largemouth Bass, Northern Pike, and Muskellunge.

References

- University Of Wisconsin Lake page [1]
- Full lake Details [2]
- U.S. Geological Survey Geographic Names Information System: East Alaska Lake [3]

Cities and Towns in Kewaunee County

Ahnapee, Wisconsin

Ahnapee, Wisconsin	
— Town —	
Location of Ahnapee, Wisconsin	
Coordinates: 44°38′2″N 87°27′50″W	
Country	United States
State	Wisconsin
County	Kewaunee
Area	
- Total	31.2 sq mi (80.7 km^2)
- Land	31.0 sq mi (80.2 km^2)
- Water	0.2 sq mi (0.5 km^2)
Elevation	587 ft (179 m)
Population (2000)	
- Total	977
- Density	31.5/sq mi (12.2/km^2)

Time zone	Central (CST) (UTC-6)
- **Summer (DST)**	CDT (UTC-5)
FIPS code	55-00600
GNIS feature ID	1582661

Ahnapee is a town in Kewaunee County, Wisconsin, United States. The population was 977 as of the 2000 Census. The unincorporated community of Rankin is located in the town.

Geography

According to the United States Census Bureau, the town has a total area of 31.2 square miles (80.7 km²), of which 31.0 square miles (80.2 km²) are land and 0.2 square mile (0.5 km²) (0.61%) is water.

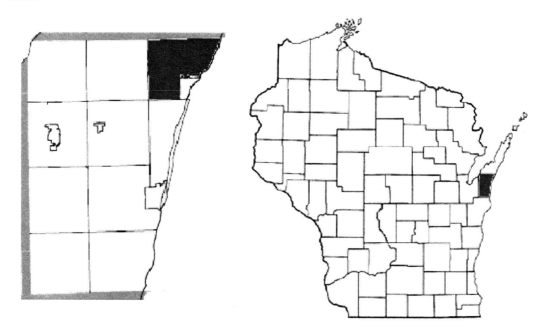

Demographics

As of the census of 2000, there were 977 people, 371 households, and 277 families residing in the town. The population density was 31.5 people per square mile (12.2/km²). There were 426 housing units at an average density of 13.8/sq mi (5.3/km²). The racial makeup of the town was 97.85% White, 0.31% African American, 0.61% Native American, 0.92% from other races, and 0.31% from two or more races. Hispanic or Latino of any race were 2.15% of the population.

There were 371 households out of which 32.1% had children under the age of 18 living with them, 67.7% were married couples living together, 3.5% had a female householder with no husband present, and 25.1% were non-families. 19.4% of all households were made up of individuals and 8.9% had someone living alone who was 65 years of age or older. The average household size was 2.63 and the average family size was 3.01.

In the town the population was spread out with 23.8% under the age of 18, 8.2% from 18 to 24, 26.9% from 25 to 44, 26.6% from 45 to 64, and 14.4% who were 65 years of age or older. The median age was 40 years. For every 100 females there were 103.1 males. For every 100 females age 18 and over, there were 105.0 males.

The median income for a household in the town was $47,500, and the median income for a family was $49,489. Males had a median income of $31,167 versus $21,518 for females. The per capita income for the town was $20,385. About 1.4% of families and 3.2% of the population were below the poverty line, including none of those under age 18 and 2.0% of those age 65 or over.

Carlton, Wisconsin

Carlton, Wisconsin	
— Town —	
Location of Carlton, Wisconsin	
Coordinates: 44°22′42″N 87°34′40″W	
Country	United States
State	Wisconsin
County	Kewaunee
Area	
- Total	35.6 sq mi (92.3 km^2)
- Land	35.6 sq mi (92.3 km^2)
- Water	0.0 sq mi (0.0 km^2)
Elevation	702 ft (214 m)
Population (2000)	
- Total	1000
- Density	28.1/sq mi (10.8/km^2)
Time zone	Central (CST) (UTC-6)
- Summer (DST)	CDT (UTC-5)
FIPS code	55-12575

Carlton, Wisconsin

| GNIS feature ID | 1582917 |

Carlton is a town in Kewaunee County, Wisconsin, United States. The population was 1,000 at the 2000 census.

Economy

The Kewaunee Nuclear Generating Station is in Carlton.

Geography

According to the United States Census Bureau, the town has a total area of 35.6 square miles (92.3 km²), all of it land.

Demographics

As of the census of 2000, there were 1,000 people, 363 households, and 283 families residing in the town. The population density was 28.1 people per square mile (10.8/km²). There were 383 housing units at an average density of 10.7/sq mi (4.2/km²). The racial makeup of the town was 99.50% White, 0.10% Pacific Islander, 0.20% from other races, and 0.20% from two or more races. Hispanic or Latino of any race were 0.20% of the population.

There were 363 households out of which 32.8% had children under the age of 18 living with them, 69.4% were married couples living together, 4.1% had a female householder with no husband present, and 22.0% were non-families. 19.6% of all households were made up of individuals and 8.8% had someone living alone who was 65 years of age or older. The average household size was 2.75 and the average family size was 3.18.

In the town the population was spread out with 25.4% under the age of 18, 7.1% from 18 to 24, 29.8% from 25 to 44, 24.6% from 45 to 64, and 13.1% who were 65 years of age or older. The median age was 38 years. For every 100 females there were 108.3 males. For every 100 females age 18 and over, there were 110.1 males.

The median income for a household in the town was $50,227, and the median income for a family was $56,094. Males had a median income of $31,667 versus $22,159 for females. The per capita income for the town was $20,660. About 2.7% of families and 3.0% of the population were below the poverty line, including 1.7% of those under age 18 and 3.8% of those age 65 or over.

Casco, Wisconsin

Casco, Wisconsin	
— Village —	
Location of Casco, Wisconsin	
Coordinates: 44°32′16″N 87°35′35″W	
Country	United States
State	Wisconsin
County	Kewaunee
Area	
- Total	1.5 sq mi (0.6 km^2)
- Land	1.5 sq mi (0.6 km^2)
- Water	0.0 sq mi (0.0 km^2)
Elevation	728 ft (222 m)
Population (2000)	
- Total	1153
- Density	32.3/sq mi (12.5/km^2)
Time zone	Central (CST) (UTC-6)
- Summer (DST)	CDT (UTC-5)
FIPS code	55-12875

| GNIS feature ID | 1582922 |

Casco is a village in Kewaunee County, Wisconsin, United States. The population was 572 at the 2000 census. It is part of the Green Bay Metropolitan Statistical Area. The village is located within the Town of Casco.

Geography

Casco is located at 44°33′15″N 87°37′14″W (44.554174, -87.620741).

According to the United States Census Bureau, the village has a total area of 0.6 square miles (1.5 km²), of which, 0.6 square miles (1.5 km²) of it is land and 1.75% is water.

Demographics

As of the census of 2000, there were 572 people, 227 households, and 162 families residing in the village. The population density was 1,022.1 people per square mile (394.4/km²). There were 236 housing units at an average density of 421.7/sq mi (162.7/km²). The racial makeup of the village was 97.55% White, 0.70% Native American, 0.87% from other races, and 0.87% from two or more races. 0.87% of the population were Hispanic or Latino of any race.

There were 227 households out of which 34.8% had children under the age of 18 living with them, 60.4% were married couples living together, 7.0% had a female householder with no husband present, and 28.2% were non-families. 25.1% of all households were made up of individuals and 12.8% had someone living alone who was 65 years of age or older. The average household size was 2.52 and the average family size was 3.01.

In the village the population was spread out with 27.1% under the age of 18, 7.2% from 18 to 24, 30.6% from 25 to 44, 18.7% from 45 to 64, and 16.4% who were 65 years of age or older. The median age was 36 years. For every 100 females there were 93.9 males. For every 100 females age 18 and over, there were 91.3 males.

The median income for a household in the village was $44,583, and the median income for a family was $50,000. Males had a median income of $36,029 versus $24,444 for females. The per capita income for the village was $18,168. About 2.8% of families and 4.0% of the population were below the poverty line, including 1.9% of those under age 18 and 9.6% of those age 65 or over.

Images

Luxemburg-Casco High School

Post office

Downtown Casco

Franklin, Kewaunee County, Wisconsin

Franklin, Wisconsin	
— Town —	
Location of Franklin, Wisconsin	
Coordinates: 44°22′0″N 87°42′55″W	
Country	United States
State	Wisconsin
County	Kewaunee
Area	
- Total	36.2 sq mi (93.7 km^2)
- Land	35.5 sq mi (91.9 km^2)
- Water	0.7 sq mi (1.8 km^2)
Elevation	804 ft (245 m)
Population (2000)	
- Total	997
- Density	28.1/sq mi (10.9/km^2)
Time zone	Central (CST) (UTC-6)
- Summer (DST)	CDT (UTC-5)
FIPS code	55-27250

| GNIS feature ID | 1583232 |

Franklin is a town in Kewaunee County, Wisconsin, United States. The population was 997 at the 2000 census.

Geography

According to the United States Census Bureau, the town has a total area of 36.2 square miles (93.7 km²), of which, 35.5 square miles (91.9 km²) of it is land and 0.7 square miles (1.8 km²) of it (1.91%) is water.

Demographics

As of the census of 2000, there were 997 people, 338 households, and 270 families residing in the town. The population density was 28.1 people per square mile (10.8/km²). There were 359 housing units at an average density of 10.1/sq mi (3.9/km²). The racial makeup of the town was 99.20% White, 0.30% African American, 0.30% Asian, 0.10% from other races, and 0.10% from two or more races. Hispanic or Latino of any race were 0.60% of the population.

There were 338 households out of which 38.5% had children under the age of 18 living with them, 67.8% were married couples living together, 6.5% had a female householder with no husband present, and 20.1% were non-families. 14.8% of all households were made up of individuals and 6.5% had someone living alone who was 65 years of age or older. The average household size was 2.95 and the average family size was 3.30.

In the town the population was spread out with 28.6% under the age of 18, 7.8% from 18 to 24, 29.0% from 25 to 44, 24.7% from 45 to 64, and 9.9% who were 65 years of age or older. The median age was 36 years. For every 100 females there were 112.6 males. For every 100 females age 18 and over, there were 117.1 males.

The median income for a household in the town was $52,019, and the median income for a family was $57,212. Males had a median income of $33,958 versus $22,237 for females. The per capita income for the town was $19,401. About 2.2% of families and 2.4% of the population were below the poverty line, including none of those under age 18 and 4.0% of those age 65 or over.

Kewaunee, Wisconsin

Kewaunee, Wisconsin	
— City —	
Location of Kewaunee, Wisconsin	
Coordinates: 44°27′32″N 87°30′34″W	
Country	United States
State	Wisconsin
County	Kewaunee
Area	
- Total	4.2 sq mi (10.9 km^2)
- Land	3.5 sq mi (9.0 km^2)
- Water	0.7 sq mi (1.9 km^2)
Elevation	610 ft (186 m)
Population (2000)	
- Total	2806
- Density	807.7/sq mi (311.9/km^2)
Time zone	Central (CST) (UTC-6)
- Summer (DST)	CDT (UTC-5)
FIPS code	55-39350
GNIS feature ID	1567445

Kewaunee is a city in Kewaunee County, Wisconsin, United States. The population was 2,806 at the 2000 census. Located on the northwestern shore of Lake Michigan, the city is the county seat of Kewaunee County.

Kewaunee is part of the Green Bay Metropolitan Statistical Area.

Kewaunee Nuclear Generating Station

Geography

Kewaunee is located at 44°27'32"N 87°30'34"W (44.458758, -87.509496).

According to the United States Census Bureau, the city has a total area of 4.2 square miles (10.9 km²), of which, 3.5 square miles (9.0 km²) of it is land and 0.7 square miles (1.9 km²) of it (17.54%) is water.

East Terminus of Highway 29 in downtown Kewaunee

Highways

- [42] WIS 42 Northbound travels to Algoma, Wisconsin. South it continues into Two Rivers and Manitowoc, Wisconsin.
- [29] WIS 29 connects with Green Bay, Wisconsin Westbound.

Demographics

As of the census of 2000, there were 2,806 people, 1,149 households, and 736 families residing in the city. The population density was 807.7 people per square mile (312.2/km²). There were 1,237 housing units at an average density of 356.1/sq mi (137.6/km²). The racial makeup of the city was 98.25% White, 0.36% African American, 0.39% Native American, 0.21% Asian, 0.14% from other races, and 0.64% from two or more races. Hispanic or Latino of any race were 0.57% of the population.

There were 1,149 households out of which 29.5% had children under the age of 18 living with them, 53.1% were married couples living together, 7.7% had a female householder with no husband present, and 35.9% were non-families. 32.6% of all households were made up of individuals and 17.6% had someone living alone who was 65 years of age or older. The average household size was 2.34 and the average family size was 2.97.

In the city the population was spread out with 23.3% under the age of 18, 7.7% from 18 to 24, 25.5% from 25 to 44, 21.7% from 45 to 64, and 21.8% who were 65 years of age or older. The median age was 41 years. For every 100 females there were 95.8 males. For every 100 females age 18 and over, there were 91.4 males.

The median income for a household in the city was $36,420, and the median income for a family was $45,643. Males had a median income of $32,292 versus $20,544 for females. The per capita income for the city was $17,384. About 11.2% of families and 10.5% of the population were below the poverty line, including 8.0% of those under age 18 and 18.0% of those age 65 or over.

Economy
- The Kewaunee Nuclear Generating Station is in Carlton in Kewaunee County.

Attractions
- Kewaunee Pierhead Lighthouse

Notable people
- Jerry Augustine, MLB player, head coach of the University of Wisconsin-Milwaukee Panthers baseball team
- Art Fiala, the last surviving World War I veteran from Wisconsin
- Terry Jorgensen, MLB player
- Thomas F. Konop, U.S. Representative
- Stan Kuick, NFL player
- Jack Novak, NFL player
- Alvin E. O'Konski, U.S. Representative
- Joseph Stika, U.S. Coast Guard Vice Admiral
- Raymond Wilding-White, composer

External links
- Kewaunee, Wisconsin website [1]

Lincoln, Kewaunee County, Wisconsin

Lincoln, Wisconsin	
— Town —	
Location of Lincoln, Wisconsin	
Coordinates: 44°37'55"N 87°35'1"W	
Country	United States
State	Wisconsin
County	Kewaunee
Area	
- Total	35.7 sq mi (92.4 km^2)
- Land	35.7 sq mi (92.4 km^2)
- Water	0.0 sq mi (0.0 km^2)
Elevation	745 ft (227 m)
Population (2000)	
- Total	957
- Density	26.8/sq mi (10.4/km^2)
Time zone	Central (CST) (UTC-6)
- Summer (DST)	CDT (UTC-5)
FIPS code	55-44425

Lincoln, Kewaunee County, Wisconsin

GNIS feature ID	1583566

Lincoln is a town in Kewaunee County, Wisconsin, United States. The population was 957 at the 2000 census. The unincorporated community of Rio Creek is located in the town. The unincorporated community of Rosiere is also located partially in the town.

Geography

According to the United States Census Bureau, the town has a total area of 35.7 square miles (92.4 km²), all of it land.

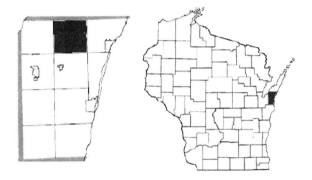

Demographics

As of the census of 2000, there were 957 people, 334 households, and 263 families residing in the town. The population density was 26.8 people per square mile (10.4/km²). There were 346 housing units at an average density of 9.7/sq mi (3.7/km²). The racial makeup of the town was 98.96% White, 0.10% African American, 0.10% Native American, 0.21% Asian, 0.10% from other races, and 0.52% from two or more races. Hispanic or Latino of any race were 1.25% of the population.

There were 334 households out of which 40.4% had children under the age of 18 living with them, 69.8% were married couples living together, 5.7% had a female householder with no husband present, and 21.0% were non-families. 17.4% of all households were made up of individuals and 10.2% had someone living alone who was 65 years of age or older. The average household size was 2.87 and the average family size was 3.23.

In the town the population was spread out with 28.5% under the age of 18, 7.6% from 18 to 24, 27.7% from 25 to 44, 23.0% from 45 to 64, and 13.2% who were 65 years of age or older. The median age was 36 years. For every 100 females there were 105.8 males. For every 100 females age 18 and over, there were 107.3 males.

The median income for a household in the town was $42,188, and the median income for a family was $45,714. Males had a median income of $32,273 versus $20,417 for females. The per capita income for the town was $16,183. About 5.9% of families and 8.9% of the population were below the poverty line, including 9.7% of those under age 18 and 7.7% of those age 65 or over.

History

Lincoln is the fourth-most Belgian-American community in the United States, by proportion of population. Lincoln was originally named "GrandLez", after the village of Grand-Leez, now a section of the town of Gembloux, Arrondissement of Namur, province of Namur, Belgium (cfr fr:Grand-Leez). Belgians emigrated from there between 1850 and 1860.

Most Belgian-American towns

- 1) Union, Door County, Wisconsin : 49 %
- 2) Red River, Wisconsin (Kewaunee County) : 47 %
- 3) Brussels, Wisconsin (Door County) : 36.4 % (composed of "Brussels community" & "Namur Community")
- 4) Lincoln, Kewaunee County, Wisconsin : 35.4 %
- 5) Green Bay, Wisconsin (Brown County) : 31.8 %

External links

- Kewaunee County [1]

References

Geographical coordinates: 44°37'05"N 87°38'31"W

Luxemburg, Wisconsin

Luxemburg, Wisconsin	
— Village —	
Location of Luxemburg, Wisconsin	
Coordinates: 44°32′45″N 87°41′39″W	
Country	United States
State	Wisconsin
County	Kewaunee
Area	
- Total	5.4 sq mi (2.1 km^2)
- Land	5.4 sq mi (2.1 km^2)
- Water	0.0 sq mi (0.0 km^2)
Elevation	791 ft (241 m)
Population (2000)	
- Total	1402
- Density	41.0/sq mi (15.8/km^2)
Time zone	Central (CST) (UTC-6)
- Summer (DST)	CDT (UTC-5)
FIPS code	55-46425
GNIS feature ID	1583611

| Website | http://luxemburgusa.com |

Luxemburg is a village in Kewaunee County, Wisconsin, United States. The population was 1,935 at the 2000 census. It is part of the Green Bay Metropolitan Statistical Area. The village is located within the town of Luxemburg.

Geography

Luxemburg is located at 44°32′18″N 87°42′17″W (44.538378, -87.704962).

Looking north at downtown Luxemburg

According to the United States Census Bureau, the village has a total area of 2.1 square miles (5.4 km²).None of the area is covered with water.

Looking east at Luxemburg

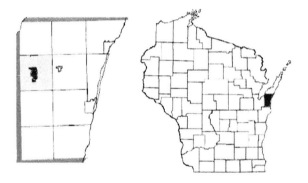

Demographics

As of the census of 2000, there were 1,935 people, 719 households, and 524 families residing in the village. The population density was 935.7 people per square mile (360.9/km²). There were 754 housing units at an average density of 364.6/sq mi (140.6/km²). The racial makeup of the village was 98.86% White, 0.10% Black or African American, 0.10% Native American, 0.26% Asian, 0.26% from other races, and 0.41% from two or more races. 0.47% of the population were Hispanic or Latino of any race.

Road sign

There were 719 households out of which 39.5% had children under the age of 18 living with them, 59.5% were married couples living together, 9.9% had a female householder with no husband present, and 27.1% were non-families. 22.7% of all households were made up of individuals and 10.4% had someone living alone who was 65 years of age or older. The average household size was 2.63 and the average family size was 3.11.

Luxemburg-Casco High School

In the village the population was spread out with 28.2% under the age of 18, 8.7% from 18 to 24, 32.8% from 25 to 44, 16.4% from 45 to 64, and 13.9% who were 65 years of age or older. The median age was 32 years. For every 100 females there were 98.7 males. For every 100 females age 18 and over, there were 89.4 males.

The median income for a household in the village was $45,000, and the median income for a family was $50,795. Males had a median income of $32,813 versus $23,897 for females. The per capita income for the village was $17,856. About 2.6% of families and 5.6% of the population were below the poverty line, including 4.8% of those under age 18 and 17.2% of those age 65 or over.

History

Luxemburg was settled in the 1850's by the Arendt and Colle families on the north end of town and the Kaut and Merens families on the south side. They came from the Grand Duchy of Luxembourg. A few years later the Daul, Peot, and Wahl families arrived from Germany.

The railroad passed through Luxemburg, connecting Sturgeon Bay, WI, and Green Bay, WI, in the early 1890s bringing growth and new business opportunities. Edward Decker conceived the idea of connecting the two cities with a rail line. It was through his efforts the Ahnapee & Western Railway Co. was formed. The line passed through wooded areas and "swampers" cleared the brush and felled trees. Any laborer handy with pick and shovel was able to secure work. Hand laborers received from $1.00 to $1.25 for a ten-hour day. A farmer with team and scraper received $3.00 per day. The first full car of freight came over the line to Ahnapee (now Algoma, WI) in September 1892. Fare was three cents a mile.

The first business in Luxemburg was erected close to the railroad tracks in 1892 by Hector Boncher, called the "Wisconsin House" soon followed in 1894 with "The Transit House" built by Desire Colle, which is known today as "The Ale House." (est.2009) The village of Luxemburg expanded rapidly with the establishment of Jule Petry's lumber yard and shingle mill in 1902. Also in 1902, telephone service arrived connecting the community with nearby business centers. Homes and stores were built, the grain elevator was erected, and the bank received its charter in 1903, giving the town a firm foundation for progress. In 1903 Nick Kaut plotted out the west side of Main Street into lots and Desire Colle, owner of the opposite side of Main Street, followed suit a year later.

About this time Dr. Felix Moraux was the first physician. Victor Kaye had charge of the Cargill elevator. Joe Rothe decided to open a furniture store, Fred Radue gave haircuts and shaves in a small building in the rear of the Wisconsin House, and Vojta Nuhlicek opened the first harness shop. A cider press was operated in back of Casper Loberger's store to quench one's thirst. In rapid order came other projects, including John Linzmeier's butcher shop, John Dupont's jewelry store and Desire Colle's tavern.

The village formed its school district in 1906 and occupied a room of the Felix VanDrisse building on Main Street with F.J. Kelliher wielding the birch rod. As Luxemburg grew the need for fire protection, street improvements, and other public services set the stage for incorporation in 1908. In 1911 the village population was 402.

In 1911 the Kewaunee branch of Green Bay & Western Railroad constructed a new turntable at Casco Junction (now the Town of Casco, WI) to handle the new Mogul locomotive, but the station was later abandoned in favor of connecting in Luxemburg. A Luxemburg station dock was constructed in 1913 and upgraded three years later with a cement platform and refrigerator compartment facilitating trade to the area.

From 1917 to 1919 some of the business establishments installed gas lighting systems for better vision. Work was started on the electric power line from Green Bay, WI to Sturgeon Bay, WI in 1920. Electricity was available for residents as of April 5, 1921. Street lights were installed on poles along the side of Main Street that same year. Citizens of Luxemburg voted for sewer and water in July 1943 and work was started in 1947 for the village pumping station. South Luxemburg requested sewer service for 14 homes, 2 taverns, St. Mary's School and a cheese factory in August 1948.

Notable people
- Benji LaCrosse, 2006 IMCA Modified national racing champion
- Matt Pell, two time NCAA Wrestling All-American champion
- Terry Jorgensen, Former Major League Baseball player

Pierce, Wisconsin

Pierce, Wisconsin	
— Town —	
Location of Pierce, Wisconsin	
Coordinates: 44°32′10″N 87°29′27″W	
Country	United States
State	Wisconsin
County	Kewaunee
Area	
- **Total**	21.8 sq mi (56.4 km^2)
- **Land**	18.6 sq mi (48.1 km^2)
- **Water**	3.2 sq mi (8.2 km^2)
Elevation	689 ft (210 m)
Population (2000)	
- **Total**	897
- **Density**	48.3/sq mi (18.6/km^2)
Time zone	Central (CST) (UTC-6)
- **Summer (DST)**	CDT (UTC-5)
FIPS code	55-62625

| GNIS feature ID | 1583920 |

Pierce is a town in Kewaunee County, Wisconsin, United States. The population was 897 at the 2000 census. The unincorporated community of Alaska is located in the town.

Geography

According to the United States Census Bureau, the town has a total area of 21.8 square miles (56.4 km²), of which, 18.6 square miles (48.1 km²) of it is land and 3.2 square miles (8.2 km²) of it (14.61%) is water.

Demographics

As of the census of 2000, there were 897 people, 329 households, and 261 families residing in the town. The population density was 48.3 people per square mile (18.6/km²). There were 407 housing units at an average density of 21.9/sq mi (8.5/km²). The racial makeup of the town was 98.10% White, 0.11% African American, 1.00% Native American, 0.11% Asian, 0.22% from other races, and 0.45% from two or more races. Hispanic or Latino of any race were 1.00% of the population.

There were 329 households out of which 33.4% had children under the age of 18 living with them, 67.5% were married couples living together, 7.6% had a female householder with no husband present, and 20.4% were non-families. 16.7% of all households were made up of individuals and 5.2% had someone living alone who was 65 years of age or older. The average household size was 2.72 and the average family size was 3.05.

In the town the population was spread out with 27.6% under the age of 18, 5.7% from 18 to 24, 26.9% from 25 to 44, 29.4% from 45 to 64, and 10.4% who were 65 years of age or older. The median age was 38 years. For every 100 females there were 108.1 males. For every 100 females age 18 and over, there were 109.4 males.

The median income for a household in the town was $43,000, and the median income for a family was $46,364. Males had a median income of $31,667 versus $23,750 for females. The per capita income for the town was $18,384. About 10.9% of families and 15.2% of the population were below the poverty line, including 26.1% of those under age 18 and 2.2% of those age 65 or over.

Counties Nearby to Visit

Door County, Wisconsin

Door County, Wisconsin	
Founded	1851
Seat	Sturgeon Bay
Area - Total - Land - Water	2370 sq mi (6138 km²) 483 sq mi (1250 km²) 1887 sq mi (4888 km²),
Population - (2000) - Density	27961 57.92/sq mi (22/km²)
Time zone	Central: UTC-6/-5
Website	www.co.door.wi.gov [1]

Door County is a county in the U.S. state of Wisconsin. As of 2000, the population was 27,961. Its county seat is Sturgeon Bay. Door County is a popular vacation and tourist destination, especially for residents of eastern Wisconsin, Upper Peninsula of Michigan, and northern Illinois.

The county is named after the strait between the Door Peninsula and Washington Island. The dangerous passage, which is now scattered with shipwrecks, was known to early French explorers and local Native Americans. Because of the natural hazards of the strait, they gave it the French appellation *Porte des Morts Passage*, which in English means the "Door to the Way to Death," or simply, "Death's Door".

Door County courthouse

Geography

The county has a total area of 6138 square kilometres (2370 sq mi). 1250 square kilometres (480 sq mi) of it is land and 4888 square kilometres (1887 sq mi) of it (79.63%) is water. The county also has more than 300 miles (480 km) of shoreline, more than almost any other in the country. This is one of the reasons that locals and tourists alike refer to the area as the *Cape Cod of the Midwest*. The county covers the majority of the Door Peninsula. With the completion of the Sturgeon Bay Shipping Canal in 1881, the northern half of the peninsula, in actuality, became an island. Limestone outcroppings, part of the Niagara Escarpment, are visible on both shores of the peninsula, but are larger and more prominent on the Green Bay side. Progressions of dunes have created much of the rest of the shoreline, especially on the easterly side. Flora along the shore provides clear evidence of plant succession. The middle of the peninsula is mostly flat or rolling cultivated land. Soils overlaying the dolomite bedrock are very thin in the northern half of the county; 39% of the County is mapped as having less than three feet to bedrock. Beyond the northern tip of the peninsula, the partially submerged ridge forms a number of islands that stretch to the Garden Peninsula in the Upper Peninsula of Michigan. The largest of these islands is Washington Island. Most of these islands form the Town of Washington.

Outcroppings at Newport State Park approximately 10 feet (3 m) from Lake Michigan

Major highways

- 42 Highway 42 (Wisconsin)
- 57 Highway 57 (Wisconsin)

Adjacent County

- Kewaunee County - south

National protected areas

- Gravel Island National Wildlife Refuge
- Green Bay National Wildlife Refuge

History

The Door County peninsula has been inhabited for about 11,000 years. Artifacts from an ancient village site at Nicolet Bay Beach have been dated to about 400 BC. This site was occupied by various cultures until about 1300 AD.

The 18th and 19th centuries saw the immigration and settlement of pioneers, mariners, fishermen and farmers. Economic sustenance came from lumbering and tourism.

During the 19th century, various groups of Native Americans occupied the area that would become Door County and its islands. Beginning in mid-century, these Indians, mostly Potawatomi, were removed from the peninsula by the federal government under the Indian Removal Act of 1830. Later in the 19th century there was a fairly large-scale immigration of Belgian Walloons, who populated a small region in the county.

A Civilian Conservation Corps camp was established at Peninsula State Park during the Great Depression. In the summer of 1945, Fish Creek was the site of a German POW camp, under an affiliation with a base camp at Fort Sheridan, Illinois. The prisoners engaged in construction projects, cut wood, and picked cherries in Peninsula State Park and the surrounding area. Eagle Bluff Lighthouse was constructed in Peninsula State Park in 1868 on orders from President Andrew Johnson, at a cost of $12,000. It was restored by the Door County Historical Society in 1964, and opened to the public.

Demographics

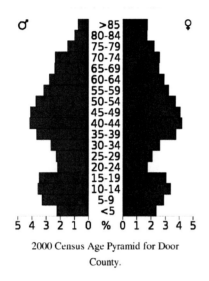

2000 Census Age Pyramid for Door County.

Historical populations		
Census	Pop.	%±
1860	2948	—
1870	4919	66.9%
1880	11645	136.7%
1890	15082	29.5%
1900	17583	16.6%
1910	18711	6.4%
1920	19073	1.9%
1930	18182	−4.7%
1940	19095	5.0%
1950	20870	9.3%
1960	20685	−0.9%

1970	20106		–2.8%
1980	25029		24.5%
1990	25690		2.6%
2000	27961		8.8%
1900-1990 [2] 1860–1890 [2]			

As of the census of 2000, there were 27,961 people, 11,828 households, and 7,995 families residing in the county. The population density was 58 people per square mile (22/km²). There were 19,587 housing units at an average density of 41 per square mile (16/km²). The racial makeup of the county was 97.84% White, 0.19% Black or African American, 0.65% Native American, 0.29% Asian, 0.01% Pacific Islander, 0.33% from other races, and 0.69% from two or more races. 0.95% of the population were Hispanic or Latino of any race. 39.4% were of German and 10.3% Belgian ancestry according to Census 2000. A small pocket of Walloon speakers is the only Walloon-language region outside of Wallonia and its immediate neighborhood.

There were 11,828 households out of which 26.90% had children under the age of 18 living with them, 58.10% were married couples living together, 6.50% had a female householder with no husband present, and 32.40% were non-families. 28.10% of all households were made up of individuals and 12.70% had someone living alone who was 65 years of age or older. The average household size was 2.33 and the average family size was 2.84.

In the county, the population was spread out with 22.10% under the age of 18, 6.10% from 18 to 24, 25.40% from 25 to 44, 27.70% from 45 to 64, and 18.70% who were 65 years of age or older. The median age was 43 years. For every 100 females there were 97.10 males. For every 100 females age 18 and over, there were 94.50 males.

Tourism

Although Door County has a year-round population of about 28,000, it experiences a tourist explosion each summer between Memorial Day and Labor Day, as the Lake Michigan spring gives way to a beautiful three month summer. Most businesses are specifically targeted to visitors, and close during the "off season". Throughout the summer, the population of Door County can reach as high as 250,000. The majority of tourists and summer residents come from the metropolitan areas of Milwaukee, Chicago, Madison, and the Twin Cities. The area is known as "the Cape Cod of the Midwest".

Door County Fairgrounds

Door County is home to five of Wisconsin's state parks: Newport State Park, northeast of Ellison Bay; Peninsula State Park, along more than six miles (10 km) of the Green Bay shoreline; Potawatomi State Park, along Sturgeon Bay; Rock Island State Park, off the tip of the Door Peninsula; and Whitefish Dunes State Park, along Lake Michigan. These five parks are known as "five jewels in the crown". They offer visitors recreational opportunities that include sightseeing, hiking, camping, swimming, fishing, and snowmobiling. Many small businesses surrounding these parks offer moped or bicycle rentals.

Cherry tree

Door County has 12 lighthouses. Most were built during the 19th century and are listed in the National Register of Historic Places: Baileys Harbor Range Lights, Cana Island Lighthouse, Chambers Island Lighthouse, Eagle Bluff Lighthouse, Pilot Island Lighthouse, Plum Island Range Lights, Pottawatomie Lighthouse, and Sturgeon Bay Canal Lighthouse. The other lighthouses in the county are: Baileys Harbor Lighthouse, Boyer Bluff Light, Sherwood Point Lighthouse, and the Sturgeon Bay Canal North Pierhead Light.

Fish Boil platter

Fish boils, offered at many Door County restaurants, are a popular meal for tourists. Potatoes, onions and whitefish from the local waters are cooked in a large kettle over a wood fire. At the end of the cooking, the cook throws fuel oil or kerosene on the fire. This "flame up" causes the water to boil over. The fish and vegetables are served with melted butter. This meal is traditionally followed by cherry pie, a traditional dessert in the area.

Door County prides itself on its cherry orchards, and a history of cherry growing that dates back to the 19th century. Soil and weather conditions - warm days and cool nights - influenced by Lake Michigan and Green Bay have created an ideal environment for growing these fruits. Many of the cherry orchards offer "pick your own cherries" along with more traditional pre-picked containers. Today with around 2200 acres (8.9 km^2) of cherry orchards and another 1000 acres (4.0 km^2) of apple orchards, Door County is filled with blossoms in the spring and richly decorated with the fruits in the late summer and fall. Montmorency cherries are usually picked from mid-July to early- to mid-August. Early varieties of apples, such as Paula Reds, are harvested as early as late August. Golden Delicious are harvested through mid-October. Cherry and apple stands can be found along many of Door County's country roads when in season. A variety of cherry products can be found in retail outlets in the county. Door County has five wineries and one microbrewery.

Door County, Wisconsin

Airports

- Door County Cherryland Airport (KSUE), located 3 miles west of Sturgeon Bay, Wisconsin
- Ephraim-Fish Creek Airport (3D2), located 1 mile southwest of Ephraim, Wisconsin

City, villages, and towns

- Baileys Harbor
- Brussels
- Clay Banks
- Egg Harbor (town)
- Egg Harbor
- Ephraim
- Forestville (town)
- Forestville
- Gardner
- Gibraltar
- Jacksonport
- Liberty Grove
- Nasewaupee
- Sevastopol
- Sister Bay
- Sturgeon Bay
- Union
- Washington

Door County, Wisconsin from the 1895 U.S. Atlas

Unincorporated communities

- Baileys Harbor
- Brussels
- Carlsville
- Carnot
- Detroit Harbor
- Ellison Bay
- Fish Creek
- Gills Rock
- Institute
- Kolberg
- Little Sturgeon
- Maplewood
- Namur
- North Bay
- Northport
- Rosiere (partial)
- Rowleys Bay
- Salona
- Valmy
- Vignes
- West Jacksonport
- Whitefish Bay

External links

- Door County Visitor Bureau [3]
- Northeast Wisconsin Historical County Plat Maps & Atlases [4] University of Wisconsin Digital Collections Center
- *History of Door County, Wisconsin* [4] (1881)
- *History of Door County, Wisconsin, The County Beautiful* [5] (1917)
- *Door County Magazine* [6]
- *Door County Style Magazine* [7] online daily news on regional arts, nature and heritage
- *Peninsula Pulse* [8] independent newspaper

Geographical coordinates: 45°01′N 87°01′W

Manitowoc County, Wisconsin

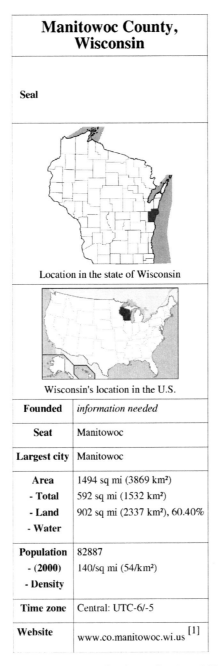

Manitowoc County, Wisconsin	
Seal	
Location in the state of Wisconsin	
Wisconsin's location in the U.S.	
Founded	*information needed*
Seat	Manitowoc
Largest city	Manitowoc
Area - Total - Land - Water	1494 sq mi (3869 km²) 592 sq mi (1532 km²) 902 sq mi (2337 km²), 60.40%
Population - (2000) - Density	82887 140/sq mi (54/km²)
Time zone	Central: UTC-6/-5
Website	www.co.manitowoc.wi.us [1]

Manitowoc County is a county in the U.S. state of Wisconsin. As of 2000, the population was 82,887. Its county seat is Manitowoc. The United States Census Bureau's Manitowoc Micropolitan Statistical

Area includes all of Manitowoc County.

Government

The County Executive is Bob Ziegelbauer, a Democrat serving a term that began with the April 2006 election. The county is also served by a 25-member County Board.

Geography

According to the U.S. Census Bureau, the county has a total area of 1,494 square miles (3,869 km²), of which 592 square miles (1,532 km²) is land and 902 square miles (2,337 km²) (60.40%) is water.

Major highways

- [57] Highway 57 (Wisconsin)
- [67] Highway 67 (Wisconsin)
- [147] Highway 147 (Wisconsin)
- [310] Highway 310 (Wisconsin)

Demographics

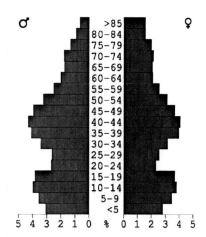

2000 Census Age Pyramid for Manitowoc County.

Historical populations		
Census	Pop.	%±
1900	42261	—
1910	44978	6.4%
1920	51644	14.8%
1930	58674	13.6%
1940	61617	5.0%
1950	67159	9.0%
1960	75215	12.0%
1970	82294	9.4%
1980	82918	0.8%
1990	80421	–3.0%
2000	82887	3.1%
WI Counties 1900-1990 [2]		

As of the census of 2000, there were 82,887 people, 32,721 households, and 22,348 families residing in the county. The population density was 140 people per square mile (54/km²). There were 34,651 housing units at an average density of 59 per square mile (23/km²). The racial makeup of the county was 95.90% White, 0.30% Black or African American, 0.43% Native American, 1.98% Asian, 0.04% Pacific Islander, 0.60% from other races, and 0.76% from two or more races. 1.62% of the population were Hispanic or Latino of any race. 53.7% were of German, 7.3% Polish, 5.3% Czech and 5.0% American ancestry according to Census 2000. 95.2% spoke English, 1.8% Spanish, 1.3% Hmong and 1.1% German as their first language.

The Manitowoc County Courthouse, listed on the National Register of Historic Places

There were 32,721 households out of which 31.50% had children under the age of 18 living with them, 57.10% were married couples living together, 7.50% had a female householder with no husband present, and 31.70% were non-families. 26.80% of all households were made up of individuals and 12.10% had someone living alone who was 65 years of age or older. The average household size was 2.49 and the average family size was 3.04.

In the county, the population was spread out with 25.50% under the age of 18, 7.60% from 18 to 24, 28.20% from 25 to 44, 23.00% from 45 to 64, and 15.70% who were 65 years of age or older. The median age was 38 years. For every 100 females there were 98.20 males. For every 100 females age 18 and over, there were 96.10 males.

Manitowoc County Expo Grounds

Cities, villages, and towns

- Cato
- Centerville
- Cleveland
- Cooperstown
- Eaton
- Francis Creek
- Franklin
- Gibson
- Kiel
- Kellnersville
- Kossuth
- Liberty
- Manitowoc Rapids
- Manitowoc (town)

Sign marking entrance to Manitowoc County in Kiel

Manitowoc County Jail

- Manitowoc
- Maple Grove
- Maribel
- Meeme
- Mishicot (town)
- Mishicot
- Newton

Manitowoc County, Wisconsin

- Reedsville
- Rockland
- Schleswig
- St. Nazianz
- Two Creeks
- Two Rivers (town)
- Two Rivers
- Valders
- Whitelaw

Unincorporated communities

- Branch
- Cato
- Clarks Mills
- Collins
- Millhome
- School Hill
- Steinthal
- Tisch Mills

Adjacent counties

- Brown County - northwest
- Kewaunee County - northeast
- Sheboygan County - south
- Calumet County - west

External links

- Manitowoc County Official Website [2]
- The Home Front: Manitowoc County in World War II [3] : The Home Front: Manitowoc County in WWII presents photographic images, oral histories, published sources, artifacts, and other resources which document the county's home front and wartime experiences from 1939 to 1947.
- Manitowoc Local History Collection [4] : Explore the history of Manitowoc and surrounding communities through more than 1,400 searchable images dating from the late 19th century through 1995. Most of the images were taken between 1890 and 1930. Peruse these images when you are doing historical or genealogical research, school assignments, business or civic presentations, or just for the fun of it! Electronic texts in this collection include:

- Plumb, Ralph Gordon. A History of Manitowoc County, 1904 [5]
- History of Manitowoc County, Wisconsin: Volume I, 1912 [6]
- History of Manitowoc County, Wisconsin: Volume II, 1912 [7]

Geographical coordinates: 44°09′N 87°33′W

Brown County, Wisconsin

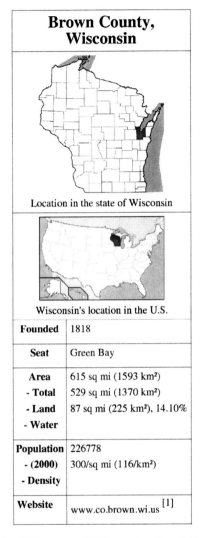

Brown County, Wisconsin	
Location in the state of Wisconsin	
Wisconsin's location in the U.S.	
Founded	1818
Seat	Green Bay
Area - Total - Land - Water	615 sq mi (1593 km²) 529 sq mi (1370 km²) 87 sq mi (225 km²), 14.10%
Population - (2000) - Density	226778 300/sq mi (116/km²)
Website	www.co.brown.wi.us [1]

Brown County is a county in the U.S. state of Wisconsin. As of 2000, the population was 226,778. The county seat is Green Bay. The United States Census Bureau's Green Bay Metropolitan Statistical Area includes all of Brown, Kewaunee, and Oconto counties.

Brown County is one of Wisconsin's two original counties along with Crawford County and originally spanned the entire eastern half of the state when formed by the Michigan Territorial legislature in 1818. It has since been subdivided to its present area. It was named for Major General Jacob Brown, a successful military leader during the War of 1812.

Geography

According to the U.S. Census Bureau, the county has a total area of 615 square miles (1592.8 km^2), of which 529 square miles (1370.1 km^2) is land and 87 square miles (225.3 km^2) (14.10%) is water.

Adjacent counties

- Oconto County – north
- Kewaunee County – east
- Manitowoc County – southeast
- Calumet County – southwest
- Outagamie County – west
- Shawano County – northwest

Major highways

- [41] U.S. Highway 41
- [141] U.S. Highway 141
- [43] Interstate 43
- [29] Highway 29 (Wisconsin)
- [32] Highway 32 (Wisconsin)
- [54] Highway 54 (Wisconsin)
- [57] Highway 57 (Wisconsin)
- [96] Highway 96 (Wisconsin)
- [172] Highway 172 (Wisconsin)
- [160] Highway 160 (Wisconsin)

Demographics

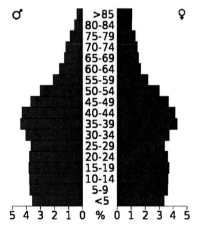

2000 Census Age Pyramid for Brown County.

Historical populations			
Census	Pop.		%±
1900	46359		—
1910	54098		16.7%
1920	61889		14.4%
1930	70249		13.5%
1940	83109		18.3%
1950	98314		18.3%
1960	125082		27.2%
1970	158244		26.5%
1980	175280		10.8%
1990	194594		11.0%
2000	226778		16.5%
WI Counties 1900-1990 [2]			

As of the census of 2000, there were 226,778 people, 87,295 households, and 57,527 families residing in the county. The population density was 429 people per square mile (166/km²). There were 90,199 housing units at an average density of 171 per square mile (66/km²). The racial makeup of the county was 91.14% White, 1.16% Black or African American, 2.29% Native American, 2.18% Asian, 0.03% Pacific Islander, 1.90% from other races, and 1.30% from two or more races. 3.84% of the population were Hispanic or Latino of any race. 33.8% were of German, 8.9% Polish, 7.8% Belgian and 6.8% Irish ancestry according to Census 2000. 93.2% spoke English, 3.8% Spanish and 1.2% Hmong as their first language.

There were 87,295 households out of which 33.90% had children under the age of 18 living with them, 53.20% were married couples living together, 8.90% had a female householder with no husband present, and 34.10% were non-families. 26.50% of all households were made up of individuals and 8.40% had someone living alone who was 65 years of age or older. The average household size was 2.51 and the average family size was 3.08.

In the county, the population was spread out with 26.10% under the age of 18, 10.50% from 18 to 24, 31.90% from 25 to 44, 20.90% from 45 to 64, and 10.70% who were 65 years of age or older. The median age was 34 years. For every 100 females there were 98.90 males. For every 100 females age 18 and over, there were 96.90 males.

Government

The legislative branch of Brown County is the 26-member Board of Supervisors. Each member represents a single member district and serves a two-year term, with elections held in the spring of even-numbered years. The Board of Supervisors elects a Chairman and Vice Chairman from its membership.

The executive branch of Brown County is the County Executive, who is elected in the Spring of every other odd-numbered year. The executive appoints department heads with the approval of the County Board. The current county executive is Tom Hinz.

Brown County has several other elected officials that are established under the Wisconsin State constitution and are referred to as the Constitutional Officers. Constitutional Officers are the only partisan elected officials within Brown County Government, as the Executive and County Board are non-partisan positions.

The current Constitutional Officers are:

- County Executive: Tom Hinz
- Clerk: Darlene Marcelle (R)
- Clerk of Circuit Courts: Lisa Wilson (D)
- District Attorney: John P. Zakowski (R)
- Register of Deeds: Cathy Williquette (D)
- Sheriff: Dennis Kocken (R)
- Treasurer: Kerry Blaney (D)

Cities, villages, and towns

Cities

- De Pere
- Green Bay

Brown County Courthouse in Green Bay

Brown County, Wisconsin

Brown County Veterans Memorial Arena

Farmland in rural Brown County

Villages

- Allouez
- Ashwaubenon
- Bellevue
- Denmark
- Hobart
- Howard
- Pulaski
- Suamico
- Wrightstown

Towns

- Eaton
- Glenmore
- Green Bay (town)
- Holland
- Humboldt
- Lawrence
- Ledgeview
- Morrison
- New Denmark
- Pittsfield
- Rockland
- Scott
- Wrightstown

Unincorporated communities

- Anston
- Askeaton
- Champion
- Dyckesville
- Fontenoy
- Greenleaf
- Hollandtown
- Lark
- Little Rapids
- New Franken
- Poland
- Shirley

External links

- Brown County website [2]
- Northeast Wisconsin Historical County Plat Maps & Atlases [4] University of Wisconsin Digital Collections Center
- *Commemorative Biographical Record of the Fox River Valley Counties of Brown, Outagamie and Winnebago* [3]

Geographical coordinates: 44°29'N 87°59'W

Things to See In and Around Kewaunee County

Algoma Pierhead Light

Algoma Pierhead Light	
Location:	Algoma, Wisconsin
Coordinates	44°36′25″N 87°25′46″W
Year first lit:	1932
Automated:	1973
Foundation:	Pier
Construction:	Steel
Tower shape:	Red cylindrical tower
Height:	48 feet (15 m)
Original lens:	Fresnel lens
Range:	16 statute miles (26 km)
Characteristic:	Red, Isophase, 6 sec. HORN: 1 blast ev 10s (1s bl). Operated from Apr. 1 to Dec. 1 and other times as required by local conditions.

The **Algoma Pierhead lighthouse** is a lighthouse located near Algoma in Kewaunee County, Wisconsin.

The lighthouse was first established in 1893 as a set of range lights. It was rebuilt in 1908 at which time it was a conical tower built of 5/16 inch steel plate, 8 feet (2.4 m) in diameter at the base and 7 feet (2.1 m) in diameter at the parapet. It stood 26 feet (7.9 m) high. In 1932 it was modified again and the entire structure was raised to a height of 42 feet (13 m) by placing the older tower on a new steel base 12 feet (3.7 m) in diameter. The original lens has been replaced by a plastic lens.

It is called **Algoma Light** and listed as number 20975 in the USCG light lists.

Images

1908 Light

Specialized additional reading

- Havighurst, Walter (1943) *The Long Ships Passing: The Story of the Great Lakes*, Macmillan Publishers.
- Oleszewski, Wes, *Great Lakes Lighthouses, American and Canadian: A Comprehensive Directory/Guide to Great Lakes Lighthouses*, (Gwinn, Michigan: Avery Color Studios, Inc., 1998) ISBN 0-932212-98-0.
- Pepper, Terry. "*Seeing the Light: Lighthouses on the western Great Lakes*" [1].
- Sapulski, Wayne S., (2001) *Lighthouses of Lake Michigan: Past and Present* (Paperback) (Fowlerville: Wilderness Adventure Books) ISBN 0923568476; ISBN 978-0923568474.
- Wright, Larry and Wright, Patricia, *Great Lakes Lighthouses Encyclopedia* Hardback (Erin: Boston Mills Press, 2006) ISBN 1-55046-399-3.

External links

- Anderson, Kraig, Lighthouse friends article [2]
- Seeing the light [3]
- Rowlett, Russ. "Lighthouses of the United States: Eastern Wisconsin" [4]. *The Lighthouse Directory*. University of North Carolina at Chapel Hill.
- National Park Service Maritime Heritage Project, Inventory of Historic Light Stations - Wisconsin [5]
- "Historic Light Station Information and Photography: Wisconsin" [6]. United States Coast Guard Historian's Office.

Gravel Island National Wildlife Refuge

Gravel Island National Wildlife Refuge	
IUCN Category IV (Habitat/Species Management Area)	
Location	Door County, Wisconsin, USA
Nearest city	Rowleys Bay
Coordinates	45°12′31″N 86°59′41″W
Area	28 acres (11 ha)
Established	1913
Governing body	U.S. Fish and Wildlife Service

Gravel Island National Wildlife Refuge is a National Wildlife Refuge located off the Door Peninsula in Wisconsin. Founded in 1913 the refuge consists of two Lake Michigan islands, that act as nesting grounds for native bird species. The refuge is part of the Wisconsin Islands Wilderness Area, and as such it is off-limits to the public to preserve the habitat of the islands. It is inhabited by large colonies of shore birds, waterfowl and also home to a pair of Great Black-backed Gulls, one of farthest westward breeding sites of the species.

History

FWS staff banding cormorants as part of tagging operations at the refuge.

In the years before the refuge's founding, multiple expeditions were made to the Islands. One Ornithologist named Henry L. Ward, then-curator of the Milwaukee Public Museum visited the area numerous times to study the Herring Gull populations. In 1906 and 1907 while visiting Gravel Island, he noted very large colonies of Herring Gulls as well as Caspian Terns, observed their behavior and collected specimens from the island. In 1913, under executive order the refuge was formed from Gravel Island and Spider Island to protect the breeding grounds of birds living there. Upon its formation it became the 29th refuge in the U.S and third in the great lakes region. In 1970 the refuge became part of the Wisconsin Islands Wilderness Area, one of the smallest in the country. Many studies have been performed at the refuge since the 1970s, and in recent times efforts have focused on migrating habits, breeding and tagging of the birds.

In 2009 the refuge became part of a Comprehensive Conservation Planning (CCP) program which will help manage the refuge more efficiently. The plan will allow for long-term continuity in refuge management, make sure that the refuge is consistent with the policies of the National Wildlife Refuge System and improve budgets for the refuge.

Geography and geology

The refuge covers 28 acres (11 ha) which comes from two islands, Spider Island spanning 23 acres (9.3 ha) and Gravel Island at a size of 4 acres (1.6 ha). The refuge is located off the east side of the Door Peninsula in Lake Michigan near Porte des Morts or "Death's Door", and is in a geographically rugged part of the Niagara Escarpment. The islands are made of mainly limestone, with little to no vegetation growing on them. They were shaped by years of receding water, powerful pre-glacial rivers, and advancing glaciers. As a result the islands are mainly flat and stick up only a few meters above the lake.

Wildlife and ecology

Flora

Spider island had a birch-cedar-tamarack forest until the late 1970s, but succumbed to the thousands of birds living on the island. The trees of Spider island have now fallen over or been washed away and no permanent vegetation is known on Gravel island.

Fauna

The refuge is home for to a wide array of bird species that either use the islands as nesting grounds or a place of shelter. The Great Black-backed Gull (*Larus marinus*) is known to have a small breeding colony on Gravel Island, and historically on Spider Island. In 1994 the species was discovered on Spider Island, making it the westernmost breeding on record at the time. Large colonies of Herring Gulls (*Larus smithsonianus*) and Double-crested Cormorants (*Phalacrocorax auritus*) are found on both islands, while a colony of Caspian Terns (*Sterna caspia*) can be found on Gravel Island. Scattered populations of waterfowl nest on Spider Island; these include the Canada Goose (*Branta canadensis*), American Black Duck (*Anas rubripes*) and Mallard (*Anas platyrhynchos*).

External links

- Park Main Page [1]

Kewaunee Pierhead Light

Kewaunee Pierhead Light	
Location:	Kewaunee, Wisconsin
Coordinates	44°27′26″N 87°29′35″W
Year first lit:	1931
Foundation:	Pier
Construction:	Steel
Tower shape:	Square
Height:	43 feet (13 m)
Original lens:	Fifth order Fresnel lens
Range:	24 kilometres (15 mi; 13 nmi)
Characteristic:	White, Flashing

The **Kewaunee Pierhead lighthouse** is a lighthouse located near Kewaunee in Kewaunee County, Wisconsin.

It replaced range lights constructed in 1891, and is located on the same pier. The fifth order fresnel lens (pronounced /freɪˈnɛl/) came from the original front range light.

The lighthouse looks nearly identical to the Holland Harbor Lighthouse, except white.

The Fresnel lens is still in operation—one of only 70 such lenses that remain operational in the United States, sixteen of which are use on the Great Lakes of which six are in Wisconsin.

Gallery

Specialized additional reading

- Havighurst, Walter (1943) *The Long Ships Passing: The Story of the Great Lakes*, Macmillan Publishers.
- Oleszewski, Wes, *Great Lakes Lighthouses, American and Canadian: A Comprehensive Directory/Guide to Great Lakes Lighthouses*, (Gwinn, Michigan: Avery Color Studios, Inc., 1998) ISBN 0-932212-98-0.
- Pepper, Terry. "*Seeing the Light: Lighthouses on the western Great Lakes*" [1].
- Sapulski, Wayne S., (2001) *Lighthouses of Lake Michigan: Past and Present* (Paperback) (Fowlerville: Wilderness Adventure Books) ISBN 0923568476; ISBN 978-0923568474.
- Wright, Larry and Wright, Patricia, *Great Lakes Lighthouses Encyclopedia* Hardback (Erin: Boston Mills Press, 2006) ISBN 1-55046-399-3.

External links

- Aerial photographs of Kewaunee Pierhead Light at Marinas.com. [1]
- Terry Pepper, Seeing the light, Kewaunee Pier light. [2]
- Lighthouse friends article [3]
- NPS Inventory of Historic Light Stations - Wisconsin [4]
- Rowlett, Russ. "Lighthouses of the United States: Eastern Wisconsin" [4]. *The Lighthouse Directory*. University of North Carolina at Chapel Hill.
- "Historic Light Station Information and Photography: Wisconsin" [6]. United States Coast Guard Historian's Office.
- (PDF) *Light List, Volume VII, Great Lakes* [5]. Light List [6]. United States Coast Guard.

Green Bay National Wildlife Refuge

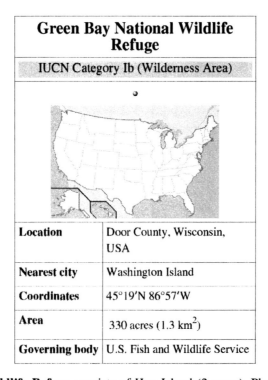

Green Bay National Wildlife Refuge	
IUCN Category Ib (Wilderness Area)	
Location	Door County, Wisconsin, USA
Nearest city	Washington Island
Coordinates	45°19′N 86°57′W
Area	330 acres (1.3 km^2)
Governing body	U.S. Fish and Wildlife Service

Green Bay National Wildlife Refuge consists of Hog Island (2 acres), Plum Island (325 acres), and Pilot Island (3.7 acres). The islands are located in Lake Michigan, near Washington Island, off the tip of Wisconsin's Door Peninsula. An Executive Order in 1913 declared Hog Island a protected breeding ground for native birds. Plum and Pilot Island were transferred from the U.S. Coast Guard to the U.S. Fish and Wildlife Service in 2007. The islands were acquired to protect native bird habitats and endangered species habitats in the Great Lakes Basin Ecosystem. Because the islands are part of the Wisconsin Islands Wilderness Area, public use of any of the islands is prohibited. The refuge is managed by staff at the Horicon National Wildlife Refuge, in Mayville, Wisconsin.

History

Great Blue Heron, one of the many birds that migrates to the Green Bay National Wildlife Refuge.

By executive order in 1913, Hog Island was declared a national preserve to provide a safe nesting and breeding ground for the species of birds native to the area. The Green Bay National Wildlife Refuge became the second national wildlife refuge in Great Lakes area. It was the 28th wildlife refuge in the United States. Gravel Island National Wildlife Refuge was also created under the same executive order. It became the 29th wildlife refuge in the United States, and the third refuge in the Great Lakes region. In 1970, Green Bay National Wildlife Refuge and Gravel Island National Wildlife Refuge were declared part of the Wisconsin Islands Wilderness Area. This wilderness area is one of the smallest in the entire United States.

Plum Island and Pilot Island originally held lighthouse facilities and provided safe havens for sailors out on Lake Michigan. Some of these safe havens are considered part of the National Register of Historic Places. By 1939, the US Coast Guard had taken control of Plum Island, and acquired control of the lighthouse on the island. The old wooden lighthouse was eventually replaced with a steel structure in 1964, and workers were moved to the island in order to oversee the operations of the lighthouse. At this time the lighthouse used range lights. By 1969, these lights were replaced with an automatic lighting system. The lighthouse is still in use today, but no longer are coast guard employees required to stay on the island to monitor the lighthouse.

The lack of human presence on the islands for many years has led to much reclamation of the land by the plants and wildlife native to the area. On October 17, 2007, Pilot and Plum Islands were officially added to the Green Bay National Wildlife Refuge. Previously under the control of the United States Coast Guard, they are now managed by the United States Fish and Wildlife Service.

Geography/Geology

The Green Bay National Wildlife Refuge consists of three main islands which cover approximately 330 acres (1.3 km^2). Hog Island covers 2 acres (8100 m^2) of land, Plum Island 325 acres (1.32 km^2), and Pilot Island approximately 3.7 acres (15000 m^2). Located off the northern tip of the Door Peninsula in Lake Michigan as part of the Niagara Escarpment, these islands are mainly composed of limestone and dolomite. These rocks form the foundations of the islands, which are a result of millions of years of compaction of sediments. The islands have been eroded and re-shaped over many years by changing water levels, specifically by the drop in water level of oceans and glacier movement.

Natural Life

Vegetation

Green Bay National Wildlife Refuge contains a variety of plants native to the area. Hog Island has an abundance of Canada yew. This plant is greatly decreasing in number on the island because of the increase in white-tailed deer and their appetite for this shrub. Other vegetation common to the wildlife refuge, specifically Hog Island, includes: red-berried elder and red raspberry plants.

Plum Island is most well known for having large forests of basswood trees and sugar maple trees, which are local to the island. Also, the coast of the island is mainly covered with white cedar trees. These trees are most commonly found in areas with an abundance of dolomite located just under the ground surface. Another plant native to the area of Plum Island is the endangered Dwarf Lake Iris (Iris Iacustris). Dwarf Lake Iris is mainly found along or near the shoreline of Plum Island.

Wildlife

Dwarf Lake Iris (Iris lacustris).

The Green Bay National Wildlife Refuge is also a safe haven for multiple species of wildlife, specifically birds. This refuge was set aside with the primary goal of protecting the native birds and other endangered species found in the Great Lakes Basin Ecosystem. Great blue herons and red-breasted mergansers are commonly found building nests and breeding at Hog Island. Large colonies of herring gulls are common, as well. These birds are able to migrate to the Green Bay National Wildlife Refuge every year due to the lack of human presence on the island. No development has occurred on Hog Island due to its small size, remoteness, and landing difficulties.

Plum Island may offer public use opportunities in the future provided they are compatible with the refuge's purpose and mission. But because no humans are currently allowed on Plum Island, the area has numerous qualities not found in the other mainland areas. One of these qualities would be the abundance of vegetation that is normally destroyed by humans. These qualities of Plum Island have resulted in the formation of a small ecosystem on the island, which has become home to many native species of birds. Pilot Island provides a safe haven for approximately 3,600 double-crested cormorant nests and almost 650 herring gull nests. Black-crowned night herons also nest on Pilot Island. Smallmouth bass, lake trout, lake sturgeon, and lake whitefish are commonly found in the waters northwest of Plum and Pilot Islands.

Wisconsin Islands Wilderness Area

In 1964, the United States Congress passed the Wilderness Act of 1964, which created the National Wilderness Preservation System. This bill declared almost 9 million acres (36000 km^2) of land across the United States federal wilderness and protected it from being overrun and destroyed by the human population. In 1970, Hog Island and Gravel Island became one of the smallest areas of land protected by the Wilderness Act, and thus became known as the Wisconsin Islands Wilderness Area.

References

This article incorporates public domain material from websites or documents of the United States Fish and Wildlife Service.

Holland Harbor Light

Holland Harbor Light	
\multicolumn{2}{c}{Holland Harbor Light}	
Location:	Ottawa County, Michigan
Coordinates	42°46′21.7″N 86°12′44.7″W
Year first lit:	1936
Automated:	1970
Foundation:	Pier
Construction:	Wood
Tower shape:	Square
Height:	32 ft (9.8 m)
Original lens:	Fourth order Fresnel lens (removed)
ARLHS number:	USA-375
USCG number:	7-19295

The **Holland Harbor Light**, known as **Big Red**, is located in Ottawa County, Michigan at the entrance of a channel connecting Lake Michigan with Lake Macatawa, and which gives access to the city of Holland, Michigan.

The lighthouse is on the south side of the channel. There are two modern lights marking the ends of the breakwaters that extend out into the Lake Michigan beyond the lighthouse.

History

After decades of local requests that went unanswered, in 1870 the United States Lighthouse Board finally recommended construction of the first light at Holland Harbor. It was thereupon approved by the U.S. Congress.

Text of the Michigan Historic Site marker:

> When seeking a location for himself and his Dutch emigrant followers in 1847, the Reverend A. C. Van Raalte was attracted by the potential of using Black Lake (Lake Macatawa) as a harbor. However, the lake's outlet to Lake Michigan was blocked by sandbars and silt. Van Raalte appealed to Congress for help. The channel was surveyed in 1849, but was not successfully opened due to inadequate appropriations. Frustrated, the Dutch settlers dug the channel themselves. On July 1, 1859, the small steamboat Huron put into port. Here, in 1886, the government established the harbor's first lifesaving station. By 1899 the channel had been relocated and harbor work completed. This spurred business and resort expansion. In 1900 over 1,095 schooners, steamers and barges used the harbor.

U.S. Coast Guard Archive Photo of original Lighthouse

> The first lighthouse built at this location was a small, square wooden structure erected in 1872. In 1880 the lighthouse service installed a new light atop a metal pole in a protective cage. The oil lantern was lowered by pulleys for service. At the turn of the century, a steel tower was built for the light and in 1907 the present structure was erected. Named the Holland Harbor South Pierhead Lighthouse, it has a gabled roof that reflects the Dutch influence in the area. The lighthouse, popularly referred to as "Big Red," was automated in 1932. When the U. S. Coast Guard recommended that it be abandoned in 1970, citizens circulated petitions to rescue it. The Holland Harbor Lighthouse Historical Commission was then organized to preserve and restore this landmark.

Except for its color, it is a virtual twin of the Kewaunee Pierhead Light on the Wisconsin side of Lake Michigan.

In 2007, the United States Department of the Interior announced that the Holland Harbor Light would be protected, making it the 12th Michigan lighthouse to have such status.

Accessibility

Public access to Big Red is somewhat limited due to the fact one must cross private property to see the lighthouse up close. However, there are no barriers for walking in to the lighthouse area. The best vantage points that are easily accessible to the general public are from across the channel at Holland State Park.

See also

- Lighthouses in the United States

Further reading

- Bibliography on Michigan lighthouses. [1]
- Crompton, Samuel Willard & Michael J. Rhein, *The Ultimate Book of Lighthouses* (2002) ISBN 1592231020; ISBN 978-1592231027.
- Hyde, Charles K., and Ann and John Mahan. *The Northern Lights: Lighthouses of the Upper Great Lakes*. Detroit: Wayne State University Press, 1995. ISBN 0814325548 ISBN 9780814325544.
- Jones, Ray & Bruce Roberts, *American Lighthouses* (Globe Pequot, September 1, 1998, 1st Ed.) ISBN 0762703245; ISBN 978-0762703241.
- Jones, Ray,*The Lighthouse Encyclopedia, The Definitive Reference* (Globe Pequot, January 1, 2004, 1st ed.) ISBN 0762727357; ISBN 978-0762727353.
- Noble, Dennis, *Lighthouses & Keepers: U. S. Lighthouse Service and Its Legacy* (Annapolis: U. S. Naval Institute Press, 1997). ISBN 1557506388; ISBN 9781557506382.
- Oleszewski, Wes, *Great Lakes Lighthouses, American and Canadian: A Comprehensive Directory/Guide to Great Lakes Lighthouses*, (Gwinn, Michigan: Avery Color Studios, Inc., 1998) ISBN 0-932212-98-0.
- Penrod, John, *Lighthouses of Michigan*, (Berrien Center, Michigan: Penrod/Hiawatha, 1998) ISBN 9780942618785 ISBN 9781893624238.
- Pepper, Terry. "*Seeing the Light: Lighthouses on the western Great Lakes*" [1].
- Putnam, George R., *Lighthouses and Lightships of the United States*, (Boston: Houghton Mifflin Co., 1933).
- United States Coast Guard, *Aids to Navigation*, (Washington, DC: U. S. Government Printing Office, 1945).
- Scott T. Price. "U. S. Coast Guard Aids to Navigation: A Historical Bibliography" [2]. United States Coast Guard Historian's Office.
- U.S. Coast Guard, *Historically Famous Lighthouses* (Washington, D.C.: Government Printing Office, 1957).

- Wagner, John L.. "*Beacons Shining in the Night: The Lighthouses of Michigan*" [3]. Clarke Historical Library, Central Michigan University.
- Wagner, John L., *Michigan Lighthouses: An Aerial Photographic Perspective*, (East Lansing, Michigan: John L. Wagner, 1998) ISBN 1880311011 ISBN 9781880311011.
- Wargin, Ed, *Legends of Light: A Michigan Lighthouse Portfolio* (Ann Arbor Media Group, 2006). ISBN 9781587262517.
- Wright, Larry and Wright, Patricia, *Great Lakes Lighthouses Encyclopedia* Hardback (Erin: Boston Mills Press, 2006) ISBN 1550463993

External links

- Detroit News, Interactive map on Michigan lighthouses. [4]
- History of Lighthouse and Holland Harbor, [5]
- Interactive map of lighthouses in southern Lake Michigan. [6]
- Lighthouse Central, Photographs, History, Directions and Way points for Holland Harbor Light, *The Ultimate Guide to West Michigan Lighthouses* by Jerry Roach (Publisher: Bugs Publishing LLC - 2005). [7] ISBN 0-9747977-0-7.
- Rowlett, Russ. "Lighthouses of the United States: Michigan's Western Lower Peninsula" [8]. *The Lighthouse Directory*. University of North Carolina at Chapel Hill.
- Lighthouse Friends (Holland Harbor Light). [9]
- Map of Michigan Lighthouse [10] in PDF Format.
- Michigan Lighthouse Conservancy, Holland Harbor Light. [11]
- National Park Service Inventory of Historic Lighthouses, Maritime Heritage, Holland Harbor (South Pierhead) lighthouse. [12]
- Terry Pepper, Seeing the Light, Holland Harbor Light, [13]
- "Historic Light Station Information and Photography: Michigan" [14]. United States Coast Guard Historian's Office.
- (PDF) *Light List, Volume VII, Great Lakes* [5]. Light List [6]. United States Coast Guard.
- Wobser, David, boatnerd.com, Holland Harbor Light. [15]

U.S. Coast Guard Archive Photo of Holland Harbor Pierhead Light

Transportation

Wisconsin Highway 29

WARNING: Article could not be rendered - ouputting plain text.

Potential causes of the problem are: (a) a bug in the pdf-writer software (b) problematic Mediawiki markup (c) table is too wide

State Trunk Highway 29Route information Maintained by WisDOTLength: 307.35 miUnited States Federal Highway Administration. "The National Highway Planning Network". . Retrieved 2007-09-02. (494.63 km)Major junctionsWest end: <!-- U.S. Highway 10 in WisconsinUS 10 / Wisconsin Highway 35WIS 35 in Prescott (WI)Prescott <!-- Wisconsin Highway 25WIS 25 in Menomonie (WI)Menomonie<!-- Interstate 94 (Wisconsin)I-94 near Elk Mound, WisconsinElk Mound<!-- U.S. Highway 53 in WisconsinUS 53 in Lake Hallie, WisconsinLake Hallie<!-- Wisconsin Highway 13WIS 13 in Abbotsford, WisconsinAbbotsford<!-- U.S. Highway 51 in WisconsinUS 51 in Wausau (WI)Wausau<!-- U.S. Highway 45 in WisconsinUS 45 in Wittenberg, WisconsinWittenberg<!-- Wisconsin Highway 22WIS 22 near Shawano (WI)Shawano<!-- U.S. Highway 41 in WisconsinUS 41 in Green Bay (WI)Green BayEast end: <!-- Wisconsin Highway 42WIS 42 in Kewaunee (WI)KewauneeHighway systemList of Wisconsin numbered highwaysWisconsin highwaysCounty Trunk Highways (Wisconsin)County • List of Wisconsin bannered routesBannered • Rustic Roads (Wisconsin)Rustic← Wisconsin Highway 28WIS 28Wisconsin Highway 30WIS 30 →For the pre-1926 Highway 29, see Highway 29 (Wisconsin 1917).State Trunk Highway 29 (often called Highway 29, STH 29 or WIS 29) is a Wisconsin State Highway systemstate highway running east–west across central Wisconsin. It is a major east–west corridor connecting the Minneapolis-St. PaulTwin Cities with Wausau, WisconsinWausau and Green Bay, WisconsinGreen Bay. A multi-year project to upgrade the corridor to a four-lane freeway/expressway from Elk Mound, WisconsinElk Mound to Green Bay was completed in 2005. The expansion served to improve safety on the route, which was over capacity as a two-lane road. The remainder of WIS 29 is two-lane surface road or urban multi-lane road.Route description East terminus in Kewaunee, WisconsinKewauneePrescott to Elk Mound WIS 29 passes through Pierce County, WisconsinPierce, St. Croix County, WisconsinSt Croix and Dunn County, WisconsinDunn Counties in this section. The highway begins at its western terminus at U.S.

Wisconsin Highway 29

Route 10 (Wisconsin)U.S. Route 10, on the north side of Prescott, WisconsinPrescott. from this point, Highway 29 follows Wisconsin Highway 35WIS 35 northeast to River Falls, WisconsinRiver Falls, passing the University of Wisconsin–River Falls campus. At the junction with Wisconsin Highway 65WIS 65, WIS 35 turns northbound with WIS 65 while WIS 29 continues east. WIS 29 joins briefly with U.S. Route 63 in WisconsinUS 63 west of Spring Valley, WisconsinSpring ValleyGoogle, Inc. Google Maps – US 63 to US 63 [map]. Cartography by Google, Inc. Retrieved 2007-12-25. and turns eastbound upon its split one mile (1.6 km) south to head into Spring Valley.Wisconsin Department of Transportation. Pierce Co [map](pdf). Retrieved 2007-12-25. Upon leaving Spring Valley and Pierce county, the route heads northward into St Croix County and turns east towards Menomonie, WisconsinMenomonie. WIS 29 does not pass through any municipalities while in this county, but it does cross Wisconsin Highway 128WIS 128.Wisconsin Department of Transportation. St. Croix Co [map](pdf). Retrieved 2007-12-25.Upon entering Dunn County, the route passes through rural terrain and enters Menomonie's west side as Hudson Rd. The route turns northward onto Main street and passes west and north of the University of Wisconsin–Stout campus. WIS 29 turns east onto Stout Road along with U.S. Route 12 in WisconsinUS 12 and leaves the city to the east.Google, Inc. Google Maps – Hudson Road, Menomonie, Wisconsin [map]. Cartography by Google, Inc. Retrieved 2007-12-25. The two routes proceed east for about 9 miles (14 km) and junction with Interstate 94. This interchange is the westernmost point of the multi-lane WIS 29 corridor.Wisconsin Department of Transportation. Dunn Co [map](pdf). Retrieved 2007-12-25. It is also the westernmost point of WIS 29 as a backbone route in Corridors 2020.Wisconsin Department of Transportation. Corridors 2020 routes: Backbones and Connectors [map](PDF). Retrieved 2007-12-25.Elk Mound to Wausau Between Elk Mound and Wausau, WisconsinWausau, WIS 29 passes through Dunn, Chippewa County, WisconsinChippewa, Clark County, WisconsinClark and Marathon County, WisconsinMarathon counties. West of CTH T, the route is an expressway. The route passes into the Eau Claire-Chippewa Falls metropolitan areaChippewa Valley metropolitan area and south of Chippewa Falls, WisconsinChippewa Falls as a Freeway and crosses U.S. Route 53 at a cloverleaf interchange in Lake Hallie, WisconsinLake Hallie.Wisconsin Department of Transportation. Chippewa Co [map](pdf). Retrieved 2007-12-25. WIS 29 junctions with the southern terminus of Wisconsin Highway 178WIS 178 southeast of Chippewa Falls then passes to the south of Lake Wissota State Park before crossing under Wisconsin Highway 27 in Cadott, WisconsinCadott. WIS 29 passes south of Boyd, WisconsinBoyd and Stanley, WisconsinStanley before exiting the county to the east.In Clark County, WIS 29 meets Wisconsin Highway 73WIS 73 in Thorp, WisconsinThorp. the two routes exit the village to the east concurrently and WIS 73 splits to the south in Withee, WisconsinWithee about 10 miles (16 km) east. WIS 29 continues east and passes south of Owen, WisconsinOwen and Curtiss, WisconsinCurtiss. At Abbotsford, WisconsinAbbotsford, WIS 29 and Wisconsin Highway 13WIS 13 meet at a partial cloverleaf interchange between Abbotsford and Colby, WisconsinColby on the Clark and Marathon county line. Twelve miles east of Abbotsford, WIS 29 and Wisconsin Highway 97WIS 97 meet at a diamond interchange. This is a key route for travelers between Wausau and Marshfield,

WisconsinMarshfield. East of this junction, WIS 29 follows a straight route that passes Edgar, WisconsinEdgar and meets Wisconsin Highway 107WIS 107 at a diamond interchange on the north side of Marathon, WisconsinMarathon City, approximately 8 miles west of Wausau. WIS 29 enters Wausau as a freeway, junctions with the western terminus of Wisconsin Highway 52WIS 52 approx. 1/2 mile west of U.S. Route 51 in WisconsinUS 51 at an eastbound off/westbound on style half-interchange. WIS 29 then immediately enters the new U.S. Route 51 in WisconsinUS 51 interchange, and turns south onto and follows U.S. Route 51 in WisconsinUS 51 for five miles (8 km), bypassing the downtown area to the south.Wisconsin Department of Transportation. Marathon Co [map](pdf). Retrieved 2007-12-25.Wausau to Green Bay WIS 29 Interchange on I-39 and US 51This stretch of the highway passes through Marathon, Shawano County, WisconsinShawano, Outagamie County, WisconsinOutagamie and Brown County, WisconsinBrown Counties. South of Wausau, WIS 29 turns off US 51 to the east at the northern terminus of Interstate 39I-39 and continues as freeway, passing through the villages of Rothschild, WisconsinRothschild and Weston, WisconsinWeston. The freeway section ends at Ringle, WisconsinRingle. As an expressway, the highway passes just south of Hatley, WisconsinHatley and turns southeast for about four miles (6 km) before turning east again at the northern terminus of Wisconsin Highway 49WIS 49.The highway enters Shawano County about one mile (1.6 km) east of this junction. WIS 29 passes north and around Wittenberg, WisconsinWittenberg. U.S. Route 45 in WisconsinUS 45 joins with the highway north of Wittenberg and the two routes run concurrently to where US 45 splits to the south at about two miles (3 km) east of the village. WIS 29 bypasses Tilleda, WisconsinTilleda and Thornton, WisconsinThornton on the way towards Shawano, WisconsinShawano At Shawano, the expressway becomes a freeway at the junction with CTH MMM (WIS 29 Business) and turns southeast to bypass Shawano to the nouth, diamond interchanges link the highway with Wisconsin Highway 22WIS 22 and Wisconsin Highway 47WIS 47 North / Wisconsin Highway 55WIS 55 North as it pass south of the city. WIS 47 South and WIS 55 South follow WIS 29 east. WIS 47 splits to the south at the diamond interchange junction with Wisconsin Highway 117WIS 117 south of Bonduel, WisconsinBonduel. WIS 29 (along with WIS 55) then returns to an expressway at the junction with CTH BE (WIS 29's former route). WIS 55 splits to the south at the diamond interchange junction with Wisconsin Highway 160WIS 160 at Angelica, WisconsinAngelica and WIS 29 heads southeast to its junction with Wisconsin Highway 156WIS 156 at the Brown County line.Wisconsin Department of Transportation. Shawano Co [map](pdf). Retrieved 2007-12-25.About one mile (1.6 km) into Brown County, WIS 29 collects Wisconsin Highway 32WIS 32 eastbound at the diamond interchange with CTH Y. WIS 29 very briefly(approx 1/2 mile!) passes through the northeast corner of Outagamie county and enters the village of Howard, WisconsinHoward. The multilane expressway and the Backbone Corridor route end at U.S. Route 41 in WisconsinUS 41.Wisconsin Department of Transportation. Brown Co [map](pdf). Retrieved 2007-12-25. WIS 32 turns south onto US 41 as WIS 29 continues into Green Bay, WisconsinGreen Bay as Shawano Avenue.Google, Inc. Google Maps – Shawano Ave, Green Bay [map]. Cartography by Google, Inc. Retrieved 2007-12-25.Green Bay to Kewaunee This section of the highway passes through Brown and

Kewaunee CountyKewaunee Counties. In downtown Green Bay, WIS 29 turns north onto South Monroe Avenue for 4 blocks, joining with Wisconsin Highway 54WIS 54 and turns east onto Main Street, splitting from WIS 54 and joining U.S. Route 141 in WisconsinUS 141 to leave the city to the southeast. The highways passes over Interstate 43I-43 without an interchange. WIS 29 splits to the east from US 141 at about 1-mile (1.6 km) north of US 141's southern terminus at I-43 in Bellevue, WisconsinBellevue. This provides the only access from I-43 to WIS 29. The highway passes through Poland, WisconsinPoland and Henrysville, WisconsinHenrysville as it exits Brown County to the east. In Kewaunee County, WIS 29 passes due east through Pilsen, WisconsinPilsen and north of Krok, WisconsinKrok as a two lane road. The highway ends in downtown Kewaunee, WisconsinKewaunee at Wisconsin Highway 42WIS 42 on the shores of Lake Michigan.Wisconsin Department of Transportation. Kewaunee Co [map](pdf). Retrieved 2007-12-25.History Prior to 1926, Highway 29 was numbered Highway 116 from Minnesota to Chippewa Falls, Highway 16 from Chippewa Falls to Bellevue (WI)Bellevue, and Highway 146 from Bellevue to Kewaunee. Highway 16 continued southeast from Bellevue along what became U.S. Highway 141 (Wisconsin)U.S. Highway 141 in 1926 to Manitowoc (WI)Manitowoc. What had been Highway 29 before 1926 became U.S. Highway 16 (Wisconsin)U.S. Highway 16 across the state. "Original State Trunk Highway System in Wisconsin". Southeast Wisconsin Regional Planning Commission. 1918. . Retrieved 2008-01-10.Highway 29 has long been known as "Bloody 29"Groves, Ethnie (2005-08-15). "Governor Doyle Officially Opens Final Segment of WIS 29 Expansion Project". Wisconsin Office of the Governor. . Retrieved 2007-06-10. because of the prevalence of grisly fatal traffic crashes along significant portions of the highway. In 1988, a study was commissioned to examine upgrading the highway to a 4-lane divided highway. The changes would be made along 203 miles (327 km) of road from I-94, 2 miles (3.2 km) west of Elk Mound, to US 41 in Howard, WisconsinHoward (suburban Green Bay, WisconsinGreen Bay). The final segment of the highway, connecting the east side of Chippewa Falls with the segment running north of Eau Claire, WisconsinEau Claire, was opened to traffic on August 16, 2005. Of the total length, about 65 miles (105 km) of the highway meets Interstate standards.Wisconsin Department of Transportation. "WIS 29 Freeway Conversion Study". . Retrieved 2007-06-10. Most of the expansion was able to be completed with only minor additions to the already-existing easements, and as a result, the expanded roadway almost exactly matches the highway's original course. While traffic crashes have declined significantly, numerous memorials to those who lost their lives on the road still dot the route. Highway 29 is the only Wisconsin state highway in WisDOT's Corridors 2020 Backbone Routes system.The portion of WIS 29 between Chippewa Falls and Abbotsford roughly follows what used to be the Yellowstone Trail "The Yellowstone Trail in Chippewa County Wisconsin". . Retrieved 2007-12-25. "The Yellowstone Trail in Clark County Wisconsin". . Retrieved 2007-12-25.In 2007, the improvements to Highway 29 won a Wonders of Wisconsin Engineering Award from the American Council of Engineering Companies, Wisconsin Chapter. Four firms (Ayres Associates, Strand Associates, CH2M Hlll and Earth Tech) were honored for their work on the project in the chapter's 50th anniversary award program. Current status Highway 29 is currently undergoing upgrades in

Wausau as a part of the US 51/WIS 29 project.Wisconsin Department of Transportation. "US-51/WI-29 Project". . Retrieved 2007-06-10. This project will expand the portions of Highway 29 that are co-signed with US 51 from 4 lanes to 6 lanes and reconstruct interchanges along the route. The southern interchange where Highway 29 turns east off from US 51 was completed in late 2006. The northern interchange where WIS 29 turns west off of US 51 is now fully open to traffic. On September 17th, 2010, the final ramp connecting WIS 29 Eastbound to US 51 northbound opened to traffic.Over the past few years, corridor preservation studies have been underway to plan for the eventual conversion of WIS 29 to full freeway standards. Areas are being studied in Marathon, Shawano, and Brown Counties. Specifically between Abbotsford and Wausau in western Marathon County, as well as from Ringle in east central Marathon County through Shawano County to CTH J in the Village of Howard in Brown County near Green Bay.Beginning in 2011, WIS 29 will be upgraded in Brown County, beginning at CTH J in the Village Of Howard, proceeding east to US 41. The WIS 29/US 41 Interchange will be upgraded to a "free-flow" freeway-to-freeway style interchange to allow for uninterrupted travel between the two highways. The upgrades will also include an interchange at CTH EB/Packerland Dr./Cardinal Ln; and a grade separated overpass at CTH J. This project is expected to last until 2015.Major intersections Prescott to Elk Mound County Location Mile Roads intersected Notes Pierce_County,_WisconsinPiercePrescott,_WisconsinPrescott<!-- U.S. Highway 10 in WisconsinUS 10 south / Wisconsin Highway 35WIS 35WIS 35 North follow WIS 29 EastRiver Falls,_WisconsinRiver Falls<!-- Wisconsin Highway 35WIS 35 north / Wisconsin Highway 65WIS 65WIS 35 South follow WIS 29 WestMartell,_WisconsinMartell<!-- U.S. Highway 63 in WisconsinUS 63St. Croix_County,_WisconsinSt. CroixSpring Valley,_WisconsinSpring Valley<!-- Wisconsin Highway 128WIS 128Dunn_County,_WisconsinDunnMenomonie,_WisconsinMenomonie<!-- U.S. Highway 12 in WisconsinUS 12 west / Wisconsin Highway 25WIS 25WIS 29 East follow US 12 East1.000 mi = 1.609 km; 1.000 km = 0.621 mi Elk Mound to Green Bay County Location Exit number#Wisconsin Department of Transportation. "Exit Numbers on WIS 29". . Retrieved 2007-06-10.Destinations Notes WIS 29 west along with US 12 (WI)US 12 west continue as a 2-lane road to Menomonie, WisconsinMenomonieDunn County, WisconsinDunnElk Mound, WisconsinElk Mound 60A-B <!-- Interstate 94 (Wisconsin)I-94 – Madison, WisconsinMadison, St. Paul, MinnesotaSt Paul Shown here as a terminus to the 4-lane expressway. WIS 29 is surface street here with a combo diamond/trumpet interchange with I-94. 61 <!-- U.S. Highway 12 in WisconsinUS 12 east / Wisconsin Highway 40WIS 40 – Colfax, WisconsinColfax, Elk Mound, WisconsinElk Mound US 12 West follow WIS 29 West. Chippewa County, WisconsinChippewaChippewa Falls, WisconsinChippewa Falls 69 <!-- CTH T 72 <!-- WIS 29 Bus. (90th Ave) 75A-B <!-- U.S. Highway 53 in WisconsinUS 53 – Eau Claire, WisconsinEau Claire, Superior, WisconsinSuperiorLake Hallie, WILake Hallie use Exit 75A; Chippewa Falls use Exit 75BTo WIS 124 use Exit 75A 79 <!-- WIS 29 Bus. / Wisconsin Highway 178WIS 178 – Chippewa Falls, WisconsinChippewa FallsSeymour Cray Sr Blvd use Exit 79 Lake Wissota, WisconsinLake Wissota 80 <!-- CTH X — Lake Wissota State Park Westbound entrance; Eastbound exit only 81 <!-- CTH J – Lake Wissota, WisconsinLake Wissota

Wisconsin Highway 29

Westbound exit; Eastbound entrance only 87 <!-- CTH X — Lake Wissota State Park Eastbound omits Lake Wissota State Park Cadott, WisconsinCadott 91 <!-- Wisconsin Highway 27WIS 27 – Cadott, WisconsinCadott, Augusta, WisconsinAugustaBoyd, WisconsinBoyd 97 <!-- CTH D – Boyd, WisconsinBoydStanley, WisconsinStanley 101 <!-- CTH H / CTH X – Stanley, WisconsinStanleyClark County, WisconsinClarkThorp, WisconsinThorp 108 <!-- Wisconsin Highway 73WIS 73 north / CTH M – Thorp, WisconsinThorpWithee, WisconsinWithee 118 <!-- Wisconsin Highway 73WIS 73 south / CTH T – Withee, WisconsinWithee, Neillsville, WisconsinNeillsvilleGreenwood, WIGreenwood use Exit 118 Owen, WisconsinOwen none <!-- CTH DD – Owen, WisconsinOwenat-grade intersection 122 <!-- CTH X (Cardinal Ave) – Owen, WisconsinOwenCurtiss, WisconsinCurtiss 127 <!-- CTH E – Curtiss, WisconsinCurtissAbbotsford, WisconsinAbbotsford 131 <!-- WIS 29 Bus. – Abbotsford, WisconsinAbbotsford Eastbound exit; Westbound entrance onlyHiline Ave use Exit 131 Marathon County, WisconsinMarathon 132 <!-- Wisconsin Highway 13WIS 13 – Colby, WisconsinColby, Abbotsford, WisconsinAbbotsfordMarshfield, WisconsinMarshfield, Medford, WisconsinMedford use Exit 132 (Marshfield only signed eastbound) 134 <!-- WIS 29 Bus. – Abbotsford, WisconsinAbbotsford Eastbound entrance; Westbound exit only Maple Rd use Exit 134 none <!-- CTH F – Cherokee, WisconsinCherokee At-grade intersection Wien, WisconsinWien 145 <!-- Wisconsin Highway 97WIS 97 – Athens, WisconsinAthens, Marshfield, WisconsinMarshfieldStratford, WisconsinStratford use Exit 145 none <!-- CTH M – Wien, WisconsinWien At-grade intersection Edgar, WisconsinEdgar 150 <!-- CTH H – Edgar, WisconsinEdgar none <!-- CTH S – Rib Falls, WisconsinRib Falls At-grade intersection Marathon City, WisconsinMarathon City 156 <!-- Wisconsin Highway 107WIS 107 – Marathon City, WisconsinMarathon City, Merrill, WisconsinMerrillWausau, WisconsinWausau 162 72nd Ave 164 A-B <!-- Wisconsin Highway 52WIS 52 (Stewart Ave) / U.S. Highway 51 in WisconsinUS 51 north – Merrill, WisconsinMerrill WIS 52/Stewart Ave, Downtown Wausau/UW Marathon County use Exit 164-AUS 51 North to Merrill use Exit 164-B*Note* WIS 52 is Eastbound exit, Westbound entrance only.Exit ramp is two lanes wide; WIS 52/Stewart Ave use left lane, US 51 North to Merrill use right lane.WIS 29 East follow US 51 South 191 (US 51) Sherman Street Northbound exit; Southbound entrance only. Rib Mountain, WisconsinRib Mountain 190 (US 51) <!-- CTH NN (North Mountain Rd) . 188 (US 51) <!-- CTH N (Rib Mountain Dr) WIS 29 West follow US 51 North 170 <!-- Interstate 39 (Wisconsin)I-39 south / U.S. Highway 51 in WisconsinUS 51 south – Stevens Point, WisconsinStevens Point, Madison, WisconsinMadison Westbound only WIS 29 Eastbound (US 51 SB)use Exit 187 towards Weston/Green Bay to continue East on WIS 29. Rothschild, WisconsinRothschild 171 <!-- US 51 Bus. – Rothschild, WisconsinRothschild, Schofield, WisconsinSchofieldWeston, WisconsinWeston 173 <!-- CTH X (Camp Phillips Rd) – Weston, WisconsinWeston 177 <!-- CTH J – Weston, WisconsinWestonRingle, WisconsinRingle 181 <!-- CTH Q – Ringle, WisconsinRingleHatley, WisconsinHatley 185 <!-- CTH Y – Hatley, WisconsinHatleyElderon, WisconsinElderon none <!-- Wisconsin Highway 49WIS 49 – Elderon, WisconsinElderon at-grade intersection Shawano County, WisconsinShawanoWittenberg,

WisconsinWittenberg 195 U.S. Highway 45 in WisconsinUS 45 north / WIS 29 Bus. / CTH M – Antigo, WisconsinAntigo, Wittenberg, WisconsinWittenberg US 45 South follows WIS 29 East 196 <!-- WIS 29 Bus. / CTH Q – Wittenberg, WisconsinWittenberg Eastbound entrance; Westbound exit only 198 U.S. Highway 45 in WisconsinUS 45 south / WIS 29 Bus. / CTH Q – Clintonville, WisconsinClintonville, Wittenberg, WisconsinWittenberg Eastbound signs omits Bus WIS 29, CTH Q, and Wittenberg US 45 North follows WIS 29 West none <!-- CTH J – Tigerton, WisconsinTigerton At-grade intersection Tilleda, WisconsinTilleda none <!-- CTH D north – Tilleda, WisconsinTilleda At-grade intersection none <!-- CTH G south none <!-- CTH D south – Leopolis, WisconsinLeopolis, Pella, WisconsinPella At-grade intersection Thornton, WisconsinThornton none <!-- CTH U – Gresham, WisconsinGresham At-grade intersection none <!-- WIS 29 Bus. / CTH MMM – Shawano, WisconsinShawano At-grade intersection Shawano, WisconsinShawano 225 <!-- Wisconsin Highway 22WIS 22 / CTH CC – Shawano, WisconsinShawano, Clintonville, WisconsinClintonville 227 Wisconsin Highway 47WIS 47 north / Wisconsin Highway 55WIS 55 north / CTH K / WIS 29 Bus. – Shawano, WisconsinShawano WIS 47 South / WIS 55 South follow WIS 29 East Bonduel, WisconsinBonduel 234 <!-- Wisconsin Highway 47WIS 47 / Wisconsin Highway 117WIS 117 – Bonduel, WisconsinBonduel, Appleton, WisconsinAppleton WIS 47 North follow WIS 29 West none <!-- CTH BE – Bonduel, WisconsinBonduel At-grade intersection - Formerly Highway 29Angelica, WisconsinAngelica none <!-- CTH F At-grade intersection none <!-- Wisconsin Highway 55WIS 55 / Wisconsin Highway 160WIS 160 – Pulaski, WisconsinPulaski, Seymour, WisconsinSeymourAngelica, WisconsinAngelica use Exit 242WIS 55 North follow WIS 29 West Brown County, WisconsinBrownPittsfield, WisconsinPittsfield none <!-- Wisconsin Highway 156WIS 156 – Pittsfield, WisconsinPittsfield At-grade intersection Oneida, WisconsinOneida 249 <!-- Wisconsin Highway 32WIS 32 / CTH V – Pulaski, WisconsinPulaski, Gillett, WisconsinGillett WIS 32 South follow WIS 29 East none <!-- CTH U At-grade intersection Green Bay, WisconsinGreen Bay none <!-- CTH C (Marley St) At-grade intersection none Greenfield Ave At-grade intersection none <!-- CTH EB (Packerland Dr) At-grade intersection none <!-- U.S. Highway 41 in WisconsinUS 41 – Marinette, WisconsinMarinette, Appleton, WisconsinAppleton WIS 32 North follow WIS 29 West Shown here as a terminus to the 4-lane expressway. WIS 29 is surface street here with a diamond interchange with the US 41 Freeway. WIS 32 follows US 41 south. Green Bay to Kewaunee County Location Mile Roads intersected Notes Brown_County,_WisconsinBrownGreen Bay,_WisconsinGreen Bay U.S. Highway 141 in WisconsinUS 141 north / Wisconsin Highway 54WIS 54 / Wisconsin Highway 57WIS 57WIS 29 East follow US 141 SouthBellevue,_WisconsinBellevue<!-- U.S. Highway 141 in WisconsinUS 141 southWIS 29 West follow US 141 NorthPoland,_WisconsinPoland<!-- CTH THenrysville,_WisconsinHenrysville<!-- CTH PKewaunee_County,_WisconsinKewauneePilsen,_WisconsinPilsen<!-- CTH VStangleville,_WisconsinStangleville<!-- CTH ABFormer State Highway 163Kewaunee,_WisconsinKewaunee<!-- Wisconsin Highway 42WIS 42WIS 29 eastern terminus1.000 mi = 1.609 km; 1.000 km = 0.621 mi Future plans WisDOT is studying options for

Highway 29 conversions to Interstate standards in three sections. The section between I-94 and County Highway X's eastern exit is already designated as a freeway by WisDOT - despite the existence of several at-grade intersections between U.S. Highway 53 (Wisconsin)U.S. Highway 53 and I-94. WisDOT is studying options for upgrade of these intersections as part of the study. In addition, upgrades to the I-94 interchange with Highway 29 are also being considered. WisDOT is also studying options for upgrades to the highway to a freeway further east to Bruce Mound Ave. in Clark County, WisconsinClark County.The second section - between Wittenberg (U.S. Highway 45 (Wisconsin)U.S. Highway 45) and Green Bay (U.S. Highway 41 (Wisconsin)U.S. Highway 41) is also undergoing a study for planned upgrades of the highway to freeway standards. As it stands now, the Shawano, WisconsinShawano bypass is the only section that is a freeway. The study is geared toward upgrading the rest of the section to Interstate standards.Wisconsin Department of Transportation (September 2005). "Project Newsletter - Wis 29 Preservation Plan: Wittenberg to Green Bay" (PDF). Archived from the original on 2007-02-21. . Retrieved 2007-06-10.The third section - between Ringle (County Highway Q) and Wittenberg (U.S. Highway 45) is at the preliminary stages for freeway upgrades. WisDOT is currently focusing on preserving right of way access for future upgrades.Wisconsin Department of Transportation. "WisDOT schedules WIS 29 public information meeting". . Retrieved 2007-06-10. Wikipedia:Link rotTo date, WisDOT has no published plans for the segments from Bruce Mound Ave. to Abbotsford (Badger Ave.) and from Abbotsford to Wausau (72nd Ave.) Bannered routes Main article: Bannered routeBannered routeMain article: Bannered routes of Wisconsin Highway 29Bannered routes of Wisconsin Highway 29 WIS 29 has four business routes: Business WIS 29 in Chippewa Falls Business WIS 29 in Abbotsford Business WIS 29 in Wittenberg Business WIS 29 in Shawano

Wisconsin Highway 42

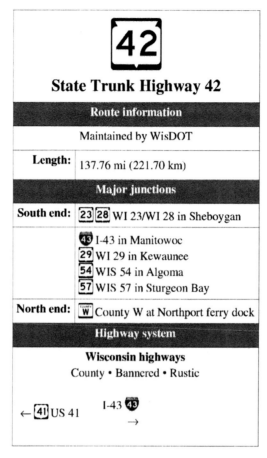

State Trunk Highway 42 (often called **Highway 42**, **STH 42** or **WIS 42**) is a state highway in the U.S. state of Wisconsin. It runs north–south in northeast Wisconsin from Northport's ferry dock to Sheboygan.

Much of the highway is part of the Lake Michigan Circle Tour (from the eastern junction with U.S. Route 10 in Manitowoc to its junction with Highway 57 in Sister Bay, Wisconsin).

Route description

WIS 42 begins at the intersection of North 14th Street and Erie Avenue (also known as Kohler Memorial Drive) in downtown Sheboygan, a block north of the bridge crossing the Sheboygan River. The intersection is the terminus of two other state highways: WIS 23 and WIS 28.

WIS 42 follows North 14th Street to Calumet Drive, which heads out of the city in a northwesterly direction to its interchange with Interstate 43 (exit 128). The route continues to the northwest into the city of Howards Grove, where it becomes Madison Avenue.

At the intersection of Madison Avenue and South Wisconsin Drive, WIS 42 and WIS 32 meet. WIS 32 continues to the northwest on Madison Avenue, while WIS 42 turns north on Wisconsin Drive. WIS 42 continues north out of Howards Grove into Manitowoc County.

WIS 42 continues to the north towards the city of Manitowoc, where it intersects with US 151 (Calumet Avenue), just west of I-43. Turning east, WIS 42 runs concurrent with US 151 for about a quarter mile before turning onto I-43 at exit 149. WIS 42 formerly ran east beyond the interchange with I-43 to South Rapids Road, following the road to the north to Waldo Boulevard and US 10 on the north side of Manitowoc. WIS 42 now runs north on I-43 to its interchange with CTH JJ (exit number 152).

WIS 42 and US 10 follow Waldo Boulevard to the shore of Lake Michigan, running northeast along the shoreline on Memorial Drive out of the city and into Two Rivers.

Crossing the West Twin River near its confluence with the East Twin River just south of downtown Two Rivers, WIS 42 becomes Washington Street. Two blocks north, it meets the eastern terminus of WIS 310 at 16th Street. Six blocks north, it meets the eastern terminus of WIS 147 at 22nd Street.

WIS 42 turns to the east on 22nd Street and crosses over the East Twin River, then turns north on Lincoln Avenue. WIS 42 and WIS 147 are the only two state highways that cross both branches of the Twin Rivers, though WIS 147 does not cross the West Twin River until about a mile east of its terminus with I-43 near Maribel.

WIS 42 continues to the north, running roughly parallel to the Lake Michigan shoreline into Kewaunee County. Just south of the city of Kewaunee, WIS 42 turns east on Krok Road to Lakeshore Drive, where it turns north and heads into the city as Milwaukee Street.

In downtown Kewaunee, WIS 42 meets the eastern terminus of another state highway, WIS 29. WIS 42 becomes Main Street after crossing the Kewaunee River and continues north out of the city.

In the unincorporated town of Alaska, WIS 42 again turns east towards Lake Michigan to follow the shoreline into Algoma as Lake Street. In downtown Algoma, WIS 42 turns north onto 4th Street and crosses the Ahnapee River. On the north bank of the river, WIS 42 turns northwest onto North Water Street and follows the river in a northerly direction to Forestville in Door County, where it becomes Forestville Avenue.

Highway 42 in Door County

Because of the geographical features and terrain of Door County, WIS 42 makes many abrupt turns as it nears its northern terminus at the tip of the Door peninsula.

At its intersection with CTH J, WIS 42 heads directly north into Door County. WIS 42 meets with WIS 57 a few miles southwest of Sturgeon Bay, and heads to the northeast with WIS 57 into the city as Green Bay Road. WIS 42 and WIS 57 are the only two state highways to enter Door County.

WIS 42 and 57 cross over the Sturgeon Bay Ship Canal to the southeast of downtown, bypassing the old Michigan Street bridge further upstream. A "Business" route continues north on Green Bay Road to South Madison Avenue, crossing the canal on the Michigan Street bridge into downtown Sturgeon Bay. Turning left to the northwest on Third Avenue, the business route follows CTH B to Jefferson Street, turning to the northeast on CTH HH. CTH HH jogs slightly north around Big Hill Park to Egg Harbor Road, where the business route turns northeast past the Door County Fairgrounds to its intersection with WIS 42 and 57 outside the city.

WIS 42 and 57 run concurrently for another mile to the north until WIS 57 turns to the East at Johns Lane. WIS 57 runs along the eastern shore of Door County until reaching its eastern terminus with WIS 42 in Sister Bay.

WIS 42 continues north on Egg Harbor Road to CTH T just west of Egg Harbor. It then swings around and along the shore of Egg Harbor before continuing to the northeast towards Fish Creek.

Outside of Fish Creek, WIS 42 takes an abrupt left-hand turn to follow the bluff down to Main Street and the Alexander Noble house. WIS 42 makes an abrupt right onto Main Street and heads to the northeast past Peninsula State Park into the unincorporated town of Eagle Harbor.

In Eagle Harbor, the road becomes Water Street as it runs along the shoreline of Green Bay. It then curves to the northeast, becoming South Bay Shore Drive outside of Sister Bay. Meeting the northern terminus of WIS 57 at Gateway Drive, WIS 42 once again swings to the northeast towards Ellison Bay.

Just outside of town, WIS 42 turns due east on School Road to its intersection with Europe Bay Road, where it turns north towards Gills Rock. At Gills Rock, WIS 42 turns due east and then turns slightly to the southeast before heading due east again to its eastern terminus at the Washington Island Ferry dock at Port Des Morts Drive in unincorporated town of Northport.

WIS 42 Spur

WIS 42 Spur is a connecting route between WIS 42 and the Island Clipper ferry in Gills Rock. The length of the spur is approximately 400 feet (120 m), the shortest highway in the Wisconsin state trunk highway system. The spur is one of three "SPUR"-designated state trunkline highways in the state along with Spur U.S. Route 51 and Spur Highway 794.

The Gills Rock ferry is a passenger-only ferry, where the one at Northport is an auto, freight and passenger ferry.

Wisconsin Highway 42

Major intersections

City	Junction	Notes
Sheboygan	WI 23/WI 28	**Beginning of road**
Erdman	I-43 - Exit# 128 on I-43	
Howards Grove	WI 32 - X Intersection	Route becomes known as Wisconsin Drive
Spring Valley	County Road XX	
Manitowoc	US-151 - Continues into Manitowoc	Route Merges with 151 for a less than 1-mile (1.6 km)
Manitowoc	I-43/WI 42 - North towards Green Bay	Route Merges with I-43/Becomes Freeway
Manitowoc	US-10/WI 42	Route Merges with US-10/End Freeway
Two Rivers	WI 147 - Towards Mishcot	
Kewaunee	WI 29 - Towards Green Bay	
Algoma	WI 54 - Known as Jefferson St.	Intersection located in Downtown Algoma
Sturgeon Bay	WI 57/WI 42	Merge/Partial Freeway
Sturgeon Bay	WI 57 - Eastern Door County	WI 57 Splits
Fish Creek	County Highway F - Towards Baileys Harbor	
Sister Bay	WI 57 - Eastern Door County	End WI 57
Northport	**End State Trunk Highway**	

Wisconsin Highway 54

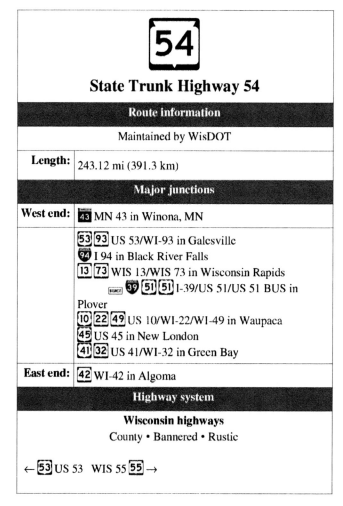

State Trunk Highway 54 (often called **Highway 54**, **STH 54** or **WIS 54**) is a Wisconsin state highway running east–west across central Wisconsin. It is 243.12 miles (391.26 km) in length.

Termini

The western terminus of Highway 54 is at the Minnesota state line at Winona, Minnesota on the North Channel Bridge. The eastern terminus is at Highway 42 in downtown Algoma at the corner of Jefferson and Lake Streets.

Municipalities served by Highway 54

- Black River Falls
- Wisconsin Rapids
- Plover
- Waupaca
- New London
- Green Bay

Images

East terminus in Algoma

West terminus

Wisconsin Highway 57

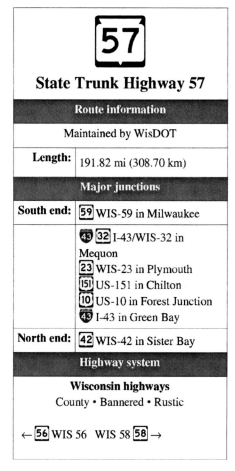

Wisconsin Highway 57 (often called **Highway 57**, **STH 57** or **WIS 57**) is a 191.82 miles (309 km) state highway in the U.S. state of Wisconsin. It runs from its southern terminus at Wisconsin Highway 59 in Milwaukee to its northern terminus at Wisconsin Highway 42 in Sister Bay. Much of WIS 57 parallels the Interstate 43 corridor, and the highway is concurrent with I-43 for 12 miles (19 km) in Ozaukee County. Like most Wisconsin state highways, WIS 57 is maintained by the Wisconsin Department of Transportation (WisDOT).

WIS 57 serves as a major highway in eastern Wisconsin, and it was originally designed to connect the major cities of Milwaukee and Green Bay as well as several other large cities along its corridor. The state of Wisconsin proposed that the WIS 57 route become an Interstate Highway corridor when the Interstate Highway System was planned in the 1950s; the state's plan was rejected in favor of the current routing of Interstate 43. WIS 57 is also a major route to the popular tourist destination of Door

County; it is one of only two state highways to serve the county.

History

When the Wisconsin State Highway system was laid out in 1918, WIS 57 ran from Racine north to Milwaukee along a route that later became U.S. Route 41 and is now Wisconsin Highway 241. By 1921, WIS 57 had been significantly expanded. It was extended northward from Milwaukee to Green Bay along what is generally its present-day route and southward from Racine to the Illinois state line. WIS 57 grew even more in 1923, when the state extended the highway northward from Green Bay to the Michigan state line. However, WIS 57 did not keep this alignment for very long. In 1927, when the U.S. Highway System was established in Wisconsin, WIS 57 was shortened at both ends. The section between Green Bay and Michigan became U.S. Route 141, and the section south of Milwaukee became part of US 41.

WIS 57 replaced WIS 78 in the Door Peninsula in 1930, reaching its present-day terminus in Sister Bay. This routing from Milwaukee to Sister Bay stayed mostly the same until the 1990s, with a few minor exceptions. WIS 57 was rerouted onto its current alignment between Hilbert and Askeaton in 1932, replacing a former routing to Holland; the original routing was replaced by county roads. The highway was also realigned between Plymouth and Kiel in 1956, and the former route became part of WIS 67.

When the federal government was planning the Interstate Highway System in the 1950s, Wisconsin proposed that the WIS 57 corridor become the route of an interstate highway. The state wanted an interstate to connect Milwaukee and Green Bay, two of Wisconsin's largest cities. Their plan chose the WIS 57 route over the nearby US 41 and US 141 corridors; the state did not want the interstate's route to favor either the port cities of Manitowoc and Sheboygan or the inland cities of Appleton, Fond du Lac and Oshkosh. Wisconsin wanted to designate the highway as Interstate 57 to preserve the highway's number; while this numbering would have fit in the west–east Interstate number scheme, an Interstate 57 was already planned in Illinois and Missouri. The state's proposal was ultimately rejected, and Interstate 43 was built on the US 141 corridor along the lakeshore instead.

WisDOT rerouted WIS 57 in south Ozaukee County during the early 1990s in response to local municipalities who complained about heavy traffic on the road. This realignment signed the highway along WIS 167 and Interstate 43 to avoid entering the downtown areas of Mequon, Thiensville, Grafton and Cedarburg. WIS 57's former routing became a municipal road. This realignment plan also turned WIS 143 over to the county and extended WIS 181 northward from WIS 167 to WIS 60.

A WisDOT project rebuilt and widened the stretch of WIS 57 between WIS 54 and WIS 42, between Sturgeon Bay and Green Bay, a primary route to the Door Peninsula, to four lanes between 1999 and 2008. This section had been a two-lane highway, but traffic during the vacation season caused long delays and made an expansion necessary. The heavy traffic also resulted in the deaths of eighteen people on this section between 1994 and 1997, earning the highway the nickname "Bloody Route 57" among locals. The project began in 1999 when the interchange between WIS 54 and WIS 57 was rebuilt as Phase I of the project. Phase 2 widened WIS 57 to four lanes on the 8 miles (13 km) between WIS 54 and Dyckesville during 2002 and 2003. The first section of four-lane road officially opened on December 2, 2003. WisDOT then began Phase 3 of the project, which widened the rest of the highway through the WIS 42 junction. The first part of this phase, a 6-mile (9.7 km) bypass of Dyckesville that reached the Door-Kewaunee county line, opened on December 1, 2006. The entire project was completed on October 6, 2008, when the last 11-mile (18 km) section near Sturgeon Bay was officially opened.

Bannered routes

Wisconsin Highway 57 has one bannered route, Wisconsin Business Highway 42/57 in Sturgeon Bay. Business Highway 42/57 is 3.55 miles (6 km) long and connects to downtown Sturgeon Bay, which WIS 42 and WIS 57 bypass. It is cosigned as a business route of both WIS 42 and WIS 57 because it splits off of the concurrency of the two highways at both of its ends. Like most auxiliary state highways in Wisconsin, Business Highway 42/57 is locally maintained.

Michigan Street Bridge

Business Route 42/57 crossed Sturgeon Bay via the Michigan Street Bridge, a historic drawbridge near downtown Sturgeon Bay, until September 2008. This bridge was built in 1930 and is 1420 feet (430 m) long. The bridge is one of only three crossings of Sturgeon Bay, the others being the WIS 42/WIS 57 bridge and the recently opened Maple and Oregon Streets Bridge. It was placed on the National Register of Historic Places on January 17, 2008. The bridge was closed to all traffic in July 2008 when structural problems were found in its supports, though it was reopened to light traffic after two days. It was again closed to all traffic when the Maple and Oregon Streets Bridge opened in September 2008, and Business Highway 42/57 was rerouted over this bridge.

Major intersections

Wisconsin Highway 57

County	Location	Mile	Junction	Notes
Milwaukee	Milwaukee	0.0	WIS 59	
		0.8	I-94	Access to Interstate 94 is via St. Paul Street
		1.5	US 18	Begin concurrency with US 18
		2.0	US 18	End concurrency with US 18
		3.1	WIS 145	
		5.2	WIS 190	Begin concurrency with WIS 190
		5.9	WIS 190	End concurrency with WIS 190
		6.0	I-43	Access to southbound I-43 only; the northbound entrance ramp can be accessed via WIS 190 and 7th Ave.
	Brown Deer	12.7	WIS 100	
Ozaukee	Thiensville	15.9	WIS 167	Begin concurrency with WIS 167
		19.1	I-43 / WIS 32 / WIS 167	Begin concurrency with I-43 and WIS 32; end concurrency with WIS 167
	Ulao	25.8	WIS 60	
	Grafton	27.1	WIS 32	End concurrency with WIS 32
	Saukville	30.4	WIS 33	
		31.4	I-43	End concurrency with I-43
	Fredonia	36.6	WIS 84	
Sheboygan	Random Lake	43.1	WIS 144	
	Waldo	50.7	WIS 28	Begin concurrency with WIS 28
		51.2	WIS 28	End concurrency with WIS 28
	Plymouth	56.3	WIS 23	
Manitowoc	Millhome	65.8	WIS 32	Begin concurrency with WIS 32
	Kiel	69.5	WIS 67	
		69.9	WIS 149	Begin concurrency with WIS 149
		70.4	WIS 149	End concurrency with WIS 149

County	Location	Mile	Road	Notes
Calumet	Chilton	80.7	<!-- 151 US 151	Begin concurrency with US 151
		81.5	<!-- 151 US 151	End concurrency with US 151
	Hilbert	87.9	<!-- 114 WIS 114	Begin concurrency with WIS 114
		89.2	<!-- 114 WIS 114	End concurrency with WIS 114
	Forest Junction	94.3	<!-- 10 US 10	
Brown	Greenleaf	102.1	<!-- 96 WIS 96	
	De Pere	111.9	<!-- 32 WIS 32	End of concurrency with WIS 32
	Allouez	114.1	<!-- 172 WIS 172	
	Green Bay	117.2	<!-- 29 54 WIS 29 / WIS 54	Beginning of concurrencies with WIS 29 and WIS 54
		117.5	<!-- 141 29 US 141 / WIS 29	End of concurrency with WIS 29
		120.2	<!-- 43 I-43	
		124.7	<!-- 54 WIS 54	
Door	Maplewood	154.2	<!-- 42 WIS 42	Begin concurrency with WIS 42
	Sturgeon Bay	165.1	<!-- 42 WIS 42	End concurrency with WIS 42
	Sister Bay	191.82	<!-- 42 WIS 42	

Article Sources and Contributors

Kewaunee County, Wisconsin *Source*: http://en.wikipedia.org/?oldid=388296442 *Contributors*: RFD

Wisconsin *Source*: http://en.wikipedia.org/?oldid=390168893 *Contributors*: Wtmitchell

Ojibwe language *Source*: http://en.wikipedia.org/?oldid=386315574 *Contributors*: Stephen G. Brown

Potawatomi language *Source*: http://en.wikipedia.org/?oldid=385059564 *Contributors*: CJLippert

West Alaska Lake *Source*: http://en.wikipedia.org/?oldid=300972567 *Contributors*: RFD

Kettle Moraine *Source*: http://en.wikipedia.org/?oldid=273331069 *Contributors*: Sift&Winnow

Krohns Lake *Source*: http://en.wikipedia.org/?oldid=302506860 *Contributors*: RFD

Green Bay (Lake Michigan) *Source*: http://en.wikipedia.org/?oldid=370510322 *Contributors*: Jhbdel

East Alaska Lake *Source*: http://en.wikipedia.org/?oldid=300972782 *Contributors*: RFD

Ahnapee, Wisconsin *Source*: http://en.wikipedia.org/?oldid=384760932 *Contributors*: Lightmouse

Carlton, Wisconsin *Source*: http://en.wikipedia.org/?oldid=369979009 *Contributors*:

Casco, Wisconsin *Source*: http://en.wikipedia.org/?oldid=379235570 *Contributors*:

Franklin, Kewaunee County, Wisconsin *Source*: http://en.wikipedia.org/?oldid=369998178 *Contributors*:

Kewaunee, Wisconsin *Source*: http://en.wikipedia.org/?oldid=378952031 *Contributors*:

Lincoln, Kewaunee County, Wisconsin *Source*: http://en.wikipedia.org/?oldid=387496702 *Contributors*:

Luxemburg, Wisconsin *Source*: http://en.wikipedia.org/?oldid=379350900 *Contributors*:

Pierce, Wisconsin *Source*: http://en.wikipedia.org/?oldid=368848274 *Contributors*:

Door County, Wisconsin *Source*: http://en.wikipedia.org/?oldid=389188009 *Contributors*: WiscoNut

Manitowoc County, Wisconsin *Source*: http://en.wikipedia.org/?oldid=386334786 *Contributors*: DCEdwards1966

Brown County, Wisconsin *Source*: http://en.wikipedia.org/?oldid=388297910 *Contributors*: RFD

Algoma Pierhead Light *Source*: http://en.wikipedia.org/?oldid=377200287 *Contributors*: Muhandes

Gravel Island National Wildlife Refuge *Source*: http://en.wikipedia.org/?oldid=384595130 *Contributors*: Iridescent

Kewaunee Pierhead Light *Source*: http://en.wikipedia.org/?oldid=377713400 *Contributors*: Muhandes

Green Bay National Wildlife Refuge *Source*: http://en.wikipedia.org/?oldid=385706866 *Contributors*: Lightmouse

Holland Harbor Light *Source*: http://en.wikipedia.org/?oldid=377489180 *Contributors*: Muhandes

Wisconsin Highway 29 *Source*: http://en.wikipedia.org/?oldid=388449101 *Contributors*:

Wisconsin Highway 42 *Source*: http://en.wikipedia.org/?oldid=368507229 *Contributors*: Imzadi1979

Wisconsin Highway 54 *Source*: http://en.wikipedia.org/?oldid=368507332 *Contributors*: Imzadi1979

Wisconsin Highway 57 *Source*: http://en.wikipedia.org/?oldid=389306329 *Contributors*:

Image Sources, Licenses and Contributors

File:Map of Wisconsin highlighting Kewaunee County.svg *Source*: http://bibliocm.bibliolabs.com/mwAnon/index.php?title=File:Map_of_Wisconsin_highlighting_Kewaunee_County.svg *License*: Public Domain *Contributors*: User:Dbenbenn

File:Map of USA WI.svg *Source*: http://bibliocm.bibliolabs.com/mwAnon/index.php?title=File:Map_of_USA_WI.svg *License*: Creative Commons Attribution 2.0 *Contributors*: Abnormaal, Hogweard, Huebi, Lokal Profil, Lupo, Mattbuck, Petr Dlouhý, 1 anonymous edits

Image:WIS 29.svg *Source*: http://bibliocm.bibliolabs.com/mwAnon/index.php?title=File:WIS_29.svg *License*: Public Domain *Contributors*: Juliancolton, Master son, SPUI

Image:WIS 42.svg *Source*: http://bibliocm.bibliolabs.com/mwAnon/index.php?title=File:WIS_42.svg *License*: Public Domain *Contributors*: Juliancolton, Rocket000, SPUI

Image:WIS 54.svg *Source*: http://bibliocm.bibliolabs.com/mwAnon/index.php?title=File:WIS_54.svg *License*: Public Domain *Contributors*: Juliancolton, SPUI

Image:WIS 57.svg *Source*: http://bibliocm.bibliolabs.com/mwAnon/index.php?title=File:WIS_57.svg *License*: Public Domain *Contributors*: Juliancolton, SPUI

Image:USA Kewaunee County, Wisconsin age pyramid.svg *Source*: http://bibliocm.bibliolabs.com/mwAnon/index.php?title=File:USA_Kewaunee_County,_Wisconsin_age_pyramid.svg *License*: Creative Commons Attribution-Sharealike 2.5 *Contributors*: user:WarX

Image:Kewaunee County.png *Source*: http://bibliocm.bibliolabs.com/mwAnon/index.php?title=File:Kewaunee_County.png *License*: Public Domain *Contributors*: US Census

Image:KewauneeCountyWisconsinWelcomeSignFarmingWIS54.jpg *Source*: http://bibliocm.bibliolabs.com/mwAnon/index.php?title=File:KewauneeCountyWisconsinWelcomeSignFarmingWIS54.jpg *License*: Creative Commons Attribution-Sharealike 3.0 *Contributors*: User:Royalbroil

Image:KewauneeWisconsinCourthouse2008.jpg *Source*: http://bibliocm.bibliolabs.com/mwAnon/index.php?title=File:KewauneeWisconsinCourthouse2008.jpg *License*: Creative Commons Attribution-Sharealike 2.5 *Contributors*: User:Royalbroil

Image:KewauneeCountyFairgroundsWisconsin.jpg *Source*: http://bibliocm.bibliolabs.com/mwAnon/index.php?title=File:KewauneeCountyFairgroundsWisconsin.jpg *License*: Creative Commons Attribution-Sharealike 2.5 *Contributors*: User:Royalbroil

File:Flag of Wisconsin.svg *Source*: http://bibliocm.bibliolabs.com/mwAnon/index.php?title=File:Flag_of_Wisconsin.svg *License*: unknown *Contributors*: Denelson83, Dual Freq, Dzordzm, Fry1989, Homo lupus, Rfc1394, Royalbroil, Svgalbertian, Zscout370, 1 anonymous edits

File:Seal of Wisconsin.svg *Source*: http://bibliocm.bibliolabs.com/mwAnon/index.php?title=File:Seal_of_Wisconsin.svg *License*: unknown *Contributors*: User:Svgalbertian

File:Map_of_USA_WI.svg *Source*: http://bibliocm.bibliolabs.com/mwAnon/index.php?title=File:Map_of_USA_WI.svg *License*: Creative Commons Attribution 2.0 *Contributors*: Abnormaal, Hogweard, Huebi, Lokal Profil, Lupo, Mattbuck, Petr Dlouhý, 1 anonymous edits

Image:Wisconsin in 1718.jpg *Source*: http://bibliocm.bibliolabs.com/mwAnon/index.php?title=File:Wisconsin_in_1718.jpg *License*: Public Domain *Contributors*: Original uploader was Billwhittaker at en.wikipedia

Image:Jean Nicolet.jpg *Source*: http://bibliocm.bibliolabs.com/mwAnon/index.php?title=File:Jean_Nicolet.jpg *License*: Public Domain *Contributors*: Original uploader was Winndm31 at en.wikipedia

Image:Birthplace of the US Republican Party 2.jpg *Source*: http://bibliocm.bibliolabs.com/mwAnon/index.php?title=File:Birthplace_of_the_US_Republican_Party_2.jpg *License*: unknown *Contributors*: Original uploader was Laharl at en.wikipedia

Image:Looking over Milwaukee from Bay View in 1882.jpg *Source*: http://bibliocm.bibliolabs.com/mwAnon/index.php?title=File:Looking_over_Milwaukee_from_Bay_View_in_1882.jpg *License*: Public Domain *Contributors*: see http://commons.wikimedia.org/wiki/File:Milwaukee_1882.jpg

Image:Chase Stone Barn - Green Grass.jpg *Source*: http://bibliocm.bibliolabs.com/mwAnon/index.php?title=File:Chase_Stone_Barn_-_Green_Grass.jpg *License*: Public Domain *Contributors*: User:KKNiteOwl

Image:Robert M. La Follette, Sr as Senator2.jpg *Source*: http://bibliocm.bibliolabs.com/mwAnon/index.php?title=File:Robert_M._La_Follette,_Sr_as_Senator2.jpg *License*: Public Domain *Contributors*: Creator: International View Co.Copyright by C.L. Wasson.

Image:Wisconsin geographic provinces.svg *Source*: http://bibliocm.bibliolabs.com/mwAnon/index.php?title=File:Wisconsin_geographic_provinces.svg *License*: Public Domain *Contributors*: User:Jua Cha

Image:Bluff.jpg *Source*: http://bibliocm.bibliolabs.com/mwAnon/index.php?title=File:Bluff.jpg *License*: Creative Commons Attribution-Sharealike 2.5 *Contributors*: User:Emery

Image:Guadalupe Shrine.jpg *Source*: http://bibliocm.bibliolabs.com/mwAnon/index.php?title=File:Guadalupe_Shrine.jpg *License*: Creative Commons Attribution 3.0 *Contributors*: User:Pgnielsen79

Image:Capitol Madison, WI.jpg *Source*: http://bibliocm.bibliolabs.com/mwAnon/index.php?title=File:Capitol_Madison,_WI.jpg *License*: Creative Commons Attribution 2.0 *Contributors*: User:Dori

Image:Milwaukee at night.jpg *Source*: http://bibliocm.bibliolabs.com/mwAnon/index.php?title=File:Milwaukee_at_night.jpg *License*: Creative Commons Attribution-Sharealike 2.0 *Contributors*: flickr user "la vaca vegetariana"

Image:Wisconsin-counties-map.gif *Source*: http://bibliocm.bibliolabs.com/mwAnon/index.php?title=File:Wisconsin-counties-map.gif *License*: Public Domain *Contributors*: Infrogmation, Semolo75, W Nowicki

File:Appletonskyline.jpg *Source*: http://bibliocm.bibliolabs.com/mwAnon/index.php?title=File:Appletonskyline.jpg *License*: unknown *Contributors*: Original uploader was Tjrudebeck at en.wikipedia

File:Eau Claire - Barstow street looking north 2005.jpg *Source*: http://bibliocm.bibliolabs.com/mwAnon/index.php?title=File:Eau_Claire_-_Barstow_street_looking_north_2005.jpg *License*: Public Domain *Contributors*: Autoshade, Urban

Image Sources, Licenses and Contributors

File:Downtown Janesville.jpg *Source*: http://bibliocm.bibliolabs.com/mwAnon/index.php?title=File:Downtown_Janesville.jpg *License*: Creative Commons Attribution-Sharealike 2.5 *Contributors*: Jeramey Jannene (w:en:User:Grassferry49Grassferry49)

File:Kenosha Harborpark 2.jpg *Source*: http://bibliocm.bibliolabs.com/mwAnon/index.php?title=File:Kenosha_Harborpark_2.jpg *License*: unknown *Contributors*: Kenokewl of English Wikipedia

File:La Crosse WI from Grandad Bluff.jpg *Source*: http://bibliocm.bibliolabs.com/mwAnon/index.php?title=File:La_Crosse_WI_from_Grandad_Bluff.jpg *License*: Creative Commons Attribution 2.0 *Contributors*: mbaylor

File:Madison Wisconsin 0210.jpg *Source*: http://bibliocm.bibliolabs.com/mwAnon/index.php?title=File:Madison_Wisconsin_0210.jpg *License*: Creative Commons Attribution-Sharealike 3.0 *Contributors*: User:Dori

File:Milwaukee_skyline.jpg *Source*: http://bibliocm.bibliolabs.com/mwAnon/index.php?title=File:Milwaukee_skyline.jpg *License*: Creative Commons Attribution 2.0 *Contributors*: Original uploader was Miwdke at en.wikipedia

File:AlgomaBlvdHistoricDistrictOshkoshWisconsin1.jpg *Source*: http://bibliocm.bibliolabs.com/mwAnon/index.php?title=File:AlgomaBlvdHistoricDistrictOshkoshWisconsin1.jpg *License*: Creative Commons Attribution-Sharealike 2.5 *Contributors*: self

File:Racine 070611.jpg *Source*: http://bibliocm.bibliolabs.com/mwAnon/index.php?title=File:Racine_070611.jpg *License*: Attribution *Contributors*: User:JeremyA

Image:Milwaukee Art Museum.jpg *Source*: http://bibliocm.bibliolabs.com/mwAnon/index.php?title=File:Milwaukee_Art_Museum.jpg *License*: GNU Free Documentation License *Contributors*: User:Sulfur

Image:Taliesin600.jpg *Source*: http://bibliocm.bibliolabs.com/mwAnon/index.php?title=File:Taliesin600.jpg *License*: Attribution *Contributors*: Original uploader was Jeff dean at en.wikipedia

Image:Summerfest Pabst Showcase 1994.jpg *Source*: http://bibliocm.bibliolabs.com/mwAnon/index.php?title=File:Summerfest_Pabst_Showcase_1994.jpg *License*: unknown *Contributors*: Original uploader was HollyAm at en.wikipedia

File:Lambeau Field panorama.jpg *Source*: http://bibliocm.bibliolabs.com/mwAnon/index.php?title=File:Lambeau_Field_panorama.jpg *License*: GNU Free Documentation License *Contributors*: Original uploader was Lordmontu at en.wikipedia

File:Miller Park.jpg *Source*: http://bibliocm.bibliolabs.com/mwAnon/index.php?title=File:Miller_Park.jpg *License*: GNU Free Documentation License *Contributors*: User Grassferry49 on en.wikipedia

File:Flag of Canada.svg *Source*: http://bibliocm.bibliolabs.com/mwAnon/index.php?title=File:Flag_of_Canada.svg *License*: Public Domain *Contributors*: User:E Pluribus Anthony, User:Mzajac

File:Flag of the United States.svg *Source*: http://bibliocm.bibliolabs.com/mwAnon/index.php?title=File:Flag_of_the_United_States.svg *License*: Public Domain *Contributors*: User:Dbenbenn, User:Indolences, User:Jacobolus, User:Technion, User:Zscout370

Image:Anishinaabewaki.jpg *Source*: http://bibliocm.bibliolabs.com/mwAnon/index.php?title=File:Anishinaabewaki.jpg *License*: Public Domain *Contributors*: Original uploader was CJLippert at en.wikipedia

File:Canadian Aboriginal Syllabics Example.svg *Source*: http://bibliocm.bibliolabs.com/mwAnon/index.php?title=File:Canadian_Aboriginal_Syllabics_Example.svg *License*: Public Domain *Contributors*: User:Vidioman

Image:Ojibwe Language Map.png *Source*: http://bibliocm.bibliolabs.com/mwAnon/index.php?title=File:Ojibwe_Language_Map.png *License*: Creative Commons Attribution 2.0 *Contributors*: Ciaurlec, Himasaram, Huhsunqu, Origamiemensch, RHorning, Shyam, Walden69, 4 anonymous edits

Image:Lakehead University Which-Way Sign.jpg *Source*: http://bibliocm.bibliolabs.com/mwAnon/index.php?title=File:Lakehead_University_Which-Way_Sign.jpg *License*: Public Domain *Contributors*: User:Vidioman

Image:20040723 Tall Ships Boating 08 Small Web view.jpg *Source*: http://bibliocm.bibliolabs.com/mwAnon/index.php?title=File:20040723_Tall_Ships_Boating_08_Small_Web_view.jpg *License*: unknown *Contributors*: Original uploader was BCantrall at en.wikipedia

File:WIMap-doton-Ahnapee.png *Source*: http://bibliocm.bibliolabs.com/mwAnon/index.php?title=File:WIMap-doton-Ahnapee.png *License*: GNU Free Documentation License *Contributors*: Original uploader was Bumm13 at en.wikipedia

File:Ahnapee.png *Source*: http://bibliocm.bibliolabs.com/mwAnon/index.php?title=File:Ahnapee.png *License*: Public Domain *Contributors*: User:Mimich

File:WIMap-doton-Carlton.png *Source*: http://bibliocm.bibliolabs.com/mwAnon/index.php?title=File:WIMap-doton-Carlton.png *License*: GNU Free Documentation License *Contributors*: Original uploader was Bumm13 at en.wikipedia

File:WIMap-doton-Casco.png *Source*: http://bibliocm.bibliolabs.com/mwAnon/index.php?title=File:WIMap-doton-Casco.png *License*: GNU Free Documentation License *Contributors*: Original uploader was Bumm13 at en.wikipedia

Image:LuxemburgCascoHighSchoolWisconsin.jpg *Source*: http://bibliocm.bibliolabs.com/mwAnon/index.php?title=File:LuxemburgCascoHighSchoolWisconsin.jpg *License*: Creative Commons Attribution-Sharealike 2.5 *Contributors*: User:Royalbroil

Image:CascoWisconsinPostOffice.jpg *Source*: http://bibliocm.bibliolabs.com/mwAnon/index.php?title=File:CascoWisconsinPostOffice.jpg *License*: Creative Commons Attribution-Sharealike 3.0 *Contributors*: User Royalbroil on en.wikipedia

Image:CascoWisconsinDowntown1.jpg *Source*: http://bibliocm.bibliolabs.com/mwAnon/index.php?title=File:CascoWisconsinDowntown1.jpg *License*: Creative Commons Attribution-Sharealike 3.0 *Contributors*: User Royalbroil on en.wikipedia

File:WIMap-doton-Franklin_b.png *Source*: http://bibliocm.bibliolabs.com/mwAnon/index.php?title=File:WIMap-doton-Franklin_b.png *License*: GNU Free Documentation License *Contributors*: Original uploader was Bumm13 at en.wikipedia

File:WIMap-doton-Kewaunee.png *Source*: http://bibliocm.bibliolabs.com/mwAnon/index.php?title=File:WIMap-doton-Kewaunee.png *License*: GNU Free Documentation License *Contributors*: Original uploader was Bumm13 at en.wikipedia

Image:KewauneeNuclearGeneratingStationAug2009.jpg *Source*: http://bibliocm.bibliolabs.com/mwAnon/index.php?title=File:KewauneeNuclearGeneratingStationAug2009.jpg *License*: Creative Commons Attribution-Sharealike 3.0 *Contributors*: User:Royalbroil

Image:WIS29EastTerminus.jpg *Source*: http://bibliocm.bibliolabs.com/mwAnon/index.php?title=File:WIS29EastTerminus.jpg *License*: Creative Commons Attribution-Sharealike 2.5 *Contributors*: Original uploader was Royalbroil at en.wikipedia

File:WIMap-doton-Lincoln_g.png *Source*: http://bibliocm.bibliolabs.com/mwAnon/index.php?title=File:WIMap-doton-Lincoln_g.png *License*: GNU Free Documentation License *Contributors*: Original uploader was Bumm13 at en.wikipedia

Image Sources, Licenses and Contributors

File:Lincoln, Kewaunee County, Wisconsin.png *Source*: http://bibliocm.bibliolabs.com/mwAnon/index.php?title=File:Lincoln,_Kewaunee_County,_Wisconsin.png *License*: Public Domain *Contributors*: User:Mimich

File:WIMap-doton-Luxemburg.png *Source*: http://bibliocm.bibliolabs.com/mwAnon/index.php?title=File:WIMap-doton-Luxemburg.png *License*: GNU Free Documentation License *Contributors*: Original uploader was Bumm13 at en.wikipedia

Image:LuxemburgWisconsinDowntown1.jpg *Source*: http://bibliocm.bibliolabs.com/mwAnon/index.php?title=File:LuxemburgWisconsinDowntown1.jpg *License*: Creative Commons Attribution-Sharealike 2.5 *Contributors*: User:Royalbroil

Image:LuxemburgWisconsinDowntown2.jpg *Source*: http://bibliocm.bibliolabs.com/mwAnon/index.php?title=File:LuxemburgWisconsinDowntown2.jpg *License*: Creative Commons Attribution-Sharealike 2.5 *Contributors*: User:Royalbroil

Image:LuxemburgWisconsinSign.jpg *Source*: http://bibliocm.bibliolabs.com/mwAnon/index.php?title=File:LuxemburgWisconsinSign.jpg *License*: Creative Commons Attribution-Sharealike 2.5 *Contributors*: User:Royalbroil

File:Luxemburg, Wisconsin.png *Source*: http://bibliocm.bibliolabs.com/mwAnon/index.php?title=File:Luxemburg,_Wisconsin.png *License*: Public Domain *Contributors*: User:Mimich

File:WIMap-doton-Pierce.png *Source*: http://bibliocm.bibliolabs.com/mwAnon/index.php?title=File:WIMap-doton-Pierce.png *License*: GNU Free Documentation License *Contributors*: Original uploader was Bumm13 at en.wikipedia

File:Map of Wisconsin highlighting Door County.svg *Source*: http://bibliocm.bibliolabs.com/mwAnon/index.php?title=File:Map_of_Wisconsin_highlighting_Door_County.svg *License*: Public Domain *Contributors*: User:Dbenbenn

Image:DoorCountyWisconsinCourthouse.jpg *Source*: http://bibliocm.bibliolabs.com/mwAnon/index.php?title=File:DoorCountyWisconsinCourthouse.jpg *License*: Creative Commons Attribution-Sharealike 3.0 *Contributors*: User:Royalbroil

Image:NiagaraEscarpmentOutcroppings_LakeMichiganShore.jpg *Source*: http://bibliocm.bibliolabs.com/mwAnon/index.php?title=File:NiagaraEscarpmentOutcroppings_LakeMichiganShore.jpg *License*: Creative Commons Attribution-Sharealike 2.5 *Contributors*: Original uploader was Royalbroil at en.wikipedia

Image:USA Door County, Wisconsin age pyramid.svg *Source*: http://bibliocm.bibliolabs.com/mwAnon/index.php?title=File:USA_Door_County,_Wisconsin_age_pyramid.svg *License*: Creative Commons Attribution-Sharealike 2.5 *Contributors*: user:WarX

File:DoorCountyWISFairgrounds.jpg *Source*: http://bibliocm.bibliolabs.com/mwAnon/index.php?title=File:DoorCountyWISFairgrounds.jpg *License*: Creative Commons Attribution-Sharealike 2.5 *Contributors*: Original uploader was Royalbroil at en.wikipedia

File:CherryTreeBalatonDoorCountyWisconsin.jpg *Source*: http://bibliocm.bibliolabs.com/mwAnon/index.php?title=File:CherryTreeBalatonDoorCountyWisconsin.jpg *License*: Creative Commons Attribution-Sharealike 3.0 *Contributors*: User:Royalbroil

File:DoorCountyWI_FishBoilPlatter.jpg *Source*: http://bibliocm.bibliolabs.com/mwAnon/index.php?title=File:DoorCountyWI_FishBoilPlatter.jpg *License*: Creative Commons Attribution-Sharealike 2.0 *Contributors*: publicprivate from Wausau, USA

Image:Door county, wisconsin, 1895.jpg *Source*: http://bibliocm.bibliolabs.com/mwAnon/index.php?title=File:Door_county,_wisconsin,_1895.jpg *License*: Public Domain *Contributors*: Feydey, Royalbroil

File:Map of Wisconsin highlighting Manitowoc County.svg *Source*: http://bibliocm.bibliolabs.com/mwAnon/index.php?title=File:Map_of_Wisconsin_highlighting_Manitowoc_County.svg *License*: Public Domain *Contributors*: User:Dbenbenn

Image:WIS 67.svg *Source*: http://bibliocm.bibliolabs.com/mwAnon/index.php?title=File:WIS_67.svg *License*: Public Domain *Contributors*: Juliancolton, SPUI

Image:WIS 147.svg *Source*: http://bibliocm.bibliolabs.com/mwAnon/index.php?title=File:WIS_147.svg *License*: Public Domain *Contributors*: Juliancolton, SPUI

Image:WIS 310.svg *Source*: http://bibliocm.bibliolabs.com/mwAnon/index.php?title=File:WIS_310.svg *License*: Public Domain *Contributors*: SPUI

Image:USA Manitowoc County, Wisconsin age pyramid.svg *Source*: http://bibliocm.bibliolabs.com/mwAnon/index.php?title=File:USA_Manitowoc_County,_Wisconsin_age_pyramid.svg *License*: Creative Commons Attribution-Sharealike 2.5 *Contributors*: user:WarX

File:ManitowocCountyCourthouseJune2010.jpg *Source*: http://bibliocm.bibliolabs.com/mwAnon/index.php?title=File:ManitowocCountyCourthouseJune2010.jpg *License*: Creative Commons Attribution-Sharealike 3.0 *Contributors*: User:Royalbroil

Image:ManitowocCountyFairgroundsWisconsin.jpg *Source*: http://bibliocm.bibliolabs.com/mwAnon/index.php?title=File:ManitowocCountyFairgroundsWisconsin.jpg *License*: Creative Commons Attribution-Sharealike 2.5 *Contributors*: Original uploader was Royalbroil at en.wikipedia

Image:ManitowocCountySignWIS57WIS32.jpg *Source*: http://bibliocm.bibliolabs.com/mwAnon/index.php?title=File:ManitowocCountySignWIS57WIS32.jpg *License*: Creative Commons Attribution-Sharealike 2.5 *Contributors*: self

File:ManitowocCountyJail.jpg *Source*: http://bibliocm.bibliolabs.com/mwAnon/index.php?title=File:ManitowocCountyJail.jpg *License*: Creative Commons Attribution-Sharealike 3.0 *Contributors*: User:Royalbroil

File:Map of Wisconsin highlighting Brown County.svg *Source*: http://bibliocm.bibliolabs.com/mwAnon/index.php?title=File:Map_of_Wisconsin_highlighting_Brown_County.svg *License*: Public Domain *Contributors*: User:Dbenbenn

Image:US 41.svg *Source*: http://bibliocm.bibliolabs.com/mwAnon/index.php?title=File:US_41.svg *License*: Public Domain *Contributors*: Rocket000, SPUI

Image:US 141.svg *Source*: http://bibliocm.bibliolabs.com/mwAnon/index.php?title=File:US_141.svg *License*: Public Domain *Contributors*: SPUI

Image:I-43.svg *Source*: http://bibliocm.bibliolabs.com/mwAnon/index.php?title=File:I-43.svg *License*: unknown *Contributors*: Augiasstallputzer, Ltljltlj, Rocket000, SPUI

Image:WIS 32.svg *Source*: http://bibliocm.bibliolabs.com/mwAnon/index.php?title=File:WIS_32.svg *License*: Public Domain *Contributors*: Juliancolton, MrDolomite, SPUI

Image:WIS 96.svg *Source*: http://bibliocm.bibliolabs.com/mwAnon/index.php?title=File:WIS_96.svg *License*: Public Domain *Contributors*: Juliancolton, SPUI

Image:WIS 172.svg *Source*: http://bibliocm.bibliolabs.com/mwAnon/index.php?title=File:WIS_172.svg *License*: Public Domain *Contributors*: Common Good, Juliancolton, SPUI

Image:WIS 160.svg *Source*: http://bibliocm.bibliolabs.com/mwAnon/index.php?title=File:WIS_160.svg *License*: Public Domain *Contributors*: Juliancolton, SPUI

Image:USA Brown County, Wisconsin age pyramid.svg *Source*: http://bibliocm.bibliolabs.com/mwAnon/index.php?title=File:USA_Brown_County,_Wisconsin_age_pyramid.svg *License*: Creative Commons Attribution-Sharealike 2.5 *Contributors*: user:WarX

Image Sources, Licenses and Contributors

File:2009-0620-GB-BrownCtyCt.jpg *Source*: http://bibliocm.bibliolabs.com/mwAnon/index.php?title=File:2009-0620-GB-BrownCtyCt.jpg *License*: Creative Commons Attribution 2.5 *Contributors*: Bobak Ha'Eri

Image:BrownCountyArenaMay2007.jpg *Source*: http://bibliocm.bibliolabs.com/mwAnon/index.php?title=File:BrownCountyArenaMay2007.jpg *License*: Creative Commons Attribution-Sharealike 2.5 *Contributors*: User Royalbroil on en.wikipedia

File:BrownCountyWisconsinBarnFarmlandSpringWIS96.jpg *Source*: http://bibliocm.bibliolabs.com/mwAnon/index.php?title=File:BrownCountyWisconsinBarnFarmlandSpringWIS96.jpg *License*: Creative Commons Attribution-Sharealike 3.0 *Contributors*: User:Royalbroil

Image:AlgomaWisconsinPierheadLighthouse2008.jpg *Source*: http://bibliocm.bibliolabs.com/mwAnon/index.php?title=File:AlgomaWisconsinPierheadLighthouse2008.jpg *License*: Creative Commons Attribution-Sharealike 2.5 *Contributors*: User:Royalbroil

Image:USCGalgoma1.JPG *Source*: http://bibliocm.bibliolabs.com/mwAnon/index.php?title=File:USCGalgoma1.JPG *License*: Public Domain *Contributors*: United States Coast Guard

Image:USCGalgoma2.JPG *Source*: http://bibliocm.bibliolabs.com/mwAnon/index.php?title=File:USCGalgoma2.JPG *License*: Public Domain *Contributors*: United States Coast Guard

Image:Green_pog.svg *Source*: http://bibliocm.bibliolabs.com/mwAnon/index.php?title=File:Green_pog *License*: Public Domain *Contributors*: Andux, Antonsusi, Juiced lemon, Rocket000, STyx, TwoWings, Wouterhagens, 3 anonymous edits

Image:US_Locator_Blank.svg *Source*: http://bibliocm.bibliolabs.com/mwAnon/index.php?title=File:US_Locator_Blank.svg *License*: GNU Free Documentation License *Contributors*: Originally uploaded English Wikipedia by and .Base versions this one is derived from: originally created by

File:Spider Island Tagging.JPG *Source*: http://bibliocm.bibliolabs.com/mwAnon/index.php?title=File:Spider_Island_Tagging.JPG *License*: Public Domain *Contributors*: Steve Lewis (U.S. Fish and Wildlife Service)

Image:KewauneeWisconsinPierheadLighthouse2008.jpg *Source*: http://bibliocm.bibliolabs.com/mwAnon/index.php?title=File:KewauneeWisconsinPierheadLighthouse2008.jpg *License*: Creative Commons Attribution-Sharealike 2.5 *Contributors*: User:Royalbroil

Image:USCGkewauneeSep.JPG *Source*: http://bibliocm.bibliolabs.com/mwAnon/index.php?title=File:USCGkewauneeSep.JPG *License*: Public Domain *Contributors*: United States Coast Guard

Image:USCGkewauneeIncorp.JPG *Source*: http://bibliocm.bibliolabs.com/mwAnon/index.php?title=File:USCGkewauneeIncorp.JPG *License*: Public Domain *Contributors*: United States Coast Guard

File:Ardea herodias NBIL.jpg *Source*: http://bibliocm.bibliolabs.com/mwAnon/index.php?title=File:Ardea_herodias_NBIL.jpg *License*: Public Domain *Contributors*: Erin Silversmith, Frank C. Müller, Howcheng, Kilom691, Malo, Mehmet Karatay, Open2universe, WikipediaMaster, Überraschungsbilder

File:Iris-lacustris.jpg *Source*: http://bibliocm.bibliolabs.com/mwAnon/index.php?title=File:Iris-lacustris.jpg *License*: unknown *Contributors*: Users Lordmaster913, JoJan on en.wikipedia

Image:PD-icon.svg *Source*: http://bibliocm.bibliolabs.com/mwAnon/index.php?title=File:PD-icon.svg *License*: Public Domain *Contributors*: User:Duesentrieb, User:Rfl

Image:Holland Harbor Lighthouse.jpg *Source*: http://bibliocm.bibliolabs.com/mwAnon/index.php?title=File:Holland_Harbor_Lighthouse.jpg *License*: GNU Free Documentation License *Contributors*: Bill Konrad (Bkonrad at en.wikipedia)

Image:Holland range mich 1913 300.jpg *Source*: http://bibliocm.bibliolabs.com/mwAnon/index.php?title=File:Holland_range_mich_1913_300.jpg *License*: Public Domain *Contributors*: United States Coast Guard

Image:Hollandharborpier 300.jpg *Source*: http://bibliocm.bibliolabs.com/mwAnon/index.php?title=File:Hollandharborpier_300.jpg *License*: Public Domain *Contributors*: United States Coast Guard

File:WIS 29.svg *Source*: http://bibliocm.bibliolabs.com/mwAnon/index.php?title=File:WIS_29.svg *License*: Public Domain *Contributors*: Juliancolton, Master son, SPUI

File:Wis-29-map.png *Source*: http://bibliocm.bibliolabs.com/mwAnon/index.php?title=File:Wis-29-map.png *License*: GNU Free Documentation License *Contributors*: User:Master_son

File:US 10.svg *Source*: http://bibliocm.bibliolabs.com/mwAnon/index.php?title=File:US_10.svg *License*: Public Domain *Contributors*: Rocket000, SPUI

File:WIS 35.svg *Source*: http://bibliocm.bibliolabs.com/mwAnon/index.php?title=File:WIS_35.svg *License*: Public Domain *Contributors*: Juliancolton, Rocket000, SPUI

File:WIS 25.svg *Source*: http://bibliocm.bibliolabs.com/mwAnon/index.php?title=File:WIS_25.svg *License*: Public Domain *Contributors*: Juliancolton, SPUI

File:I-94.svg *Source*: http://bibliocm.bibliolabs.com/mwAnon/index.php?title=File:I-94.svg *License*: unknown *Contributors*: Augiasstallputzer, Ltljltlj, SPUI, 1 anonymous edits

File:US 53.svg *Source*: http://bibliocm.bibliolabs.com/mwAnon/index.php?title=File:US_53.svg *License*: Public Domain *Contributors*: Rocket000, SPUI

File:WIS 13.svg *Source*: http://bibliocm.bibliolabs.com/mwAnon/index.php?title=File:WIS_13.svg *License*: Public Domain *Contributors*: Juliancolton, SPUI

File:US 51.svg *Source*: http://bibliocm.bibliolabs.com/mwAnon/index.php?title=File:US_51.svg *License*: Public Domain *Contributors*: Bidgee, SPUI, 3 anonymous edits

File:US 45.svg *Source*: http://bibliocm.bibliolabs.com/mwAnon/index.php?title=File:US_45.svg *License*: Public Domain *Contributors*: Luigi Chiesa, SPUI, Xnatedawgx

File:WIS 22.svg *Source*: http://bibliocm.bibliolabs.com/mwAnon/index.php?title=File:WIS_22.svg *License*: Public Domain *Contributors*: Juliancolton, SPUI

File:US 41.svg *Source*: http://bibliocm.bibliolabs.com/mwAnon/index.php?title=File:US_41.svg *License*: Public Domain *Contributors*: Rocket000, SPUI

File:WIS 42.svg *Source*: http://bibliocm.bibliolabs.com/mwAnon/index.php?title=File:WIS_42.svg *License*: Public Domain *Contributors*: Juliancolton, Rocket000, SPUI

File:WIS 28.svg *Source*: http://bibliocm.bibliolabs.com/mwAnon/index.php?title=File:WIS_28.svg *License*: Public Domain *Contributors*: User:SPUI

File:WIS 30.svg *Source*: http://bibliocm.bibliolabs.com/mwAnon/index.php?title=File:WIS_30.svg *License*: Public Domain *Contributors*: SPUI

File:US 51 WI 29 East Wausau.png *Source*: http://bibliocm.bibliolabs.com/mwAnon/index.php?title=File:US_51_WI_29_East_Wausau.png *License*: GNU Free Documentation License *Contributors*: User: Master son

File:WIS 65.svg *Source*: http://bibliocm.bibliolabs.com/mwAnon/index.php?title=File:WIS_65.svg *License*: Public Domain *Contributors*: SPUI

File:US 63.svg *Source*: http://bibliocm.bibliolabs.com/mwAnon/index.php?title=File:US_63.svg *License*: Public Domain *Contributors*: Bidgee, SPUI, 3 anonymous edits

File:WIS 128.svg *Source*: http://bibliocm.bibliolabs.com/mwAnon/index.php?title=File:WIS_128.svg *License*: Public Domain *Contributors*: Kanonkas, SPUI

File:US 12.svg *Source*: http://bibliocm.bibliolabs.com/mwAnon/index.php?title=File:US_12.svg *License*: Public Domain *Contributors*: Bidgee, SPUI, 3 anonymous edits

File:WIS 40.svg *Source*: http://bibliocm.bibliolabs.com/mwAnon/index.php?title=File:WIS_40.svg *License*: Public Domain *Contributors*: SPUI

Image Sources, Licenses and Contributors

File:WIS County T.svg *Source*: http://bibliocm.bibliolabs.com/mwAnon/index.php?title=File:WIS_County_T.svg *License*: Public Domain *Contributors*: SPUI

Image:Business plate.svg *Source*: http://bibliocm.bibliolabs.com/mwAnon/index.php?title=File:Business_plate.svg *License*: unknown *Contributors*: Homefryes, Ltljltlj, RTCNCA, SPUI

Image:no image wide.svg *Source*: http://bibliocm.bibliolabs.com/mwAnon/index.php?title=File:No_image_wide.svg *License*: Public Domain *Contributors*: SPUI, TwinsMetsFan

File:WIS 178.svg *Source*: http://bibliocm.bibliolabs.com/mwAnon/index.php?title=File:WIS_178.svg *License*: Public Domain *Contributors*: Common Good, SPUI

File:WIS County X.svg *Source*: http://bibliocm.bibliolabs.com/mwAnon/index.php?title=File:WIS_County_X.svg *License*: Public Domain *Contributors*: SPUI

File:WIS County J.svg *Source*: http://bibliocm.bibliolabs.com/mwAnon/index.php?title=File:WIS_County_J.svg *License*: Public Domain *Contributors*: Rocket000, SPUI

File:WIS 27.svg *Source*: http://bibliocm.bibliolabs.com/mwAnon/index.php?title=File:WIS_27.svg *License*: Public Domain *Contributors*: user:spui

File:WIS County D.svg *Source*: http://bibliocm.bibliolabs.com/mwAnon/index.php?title=File:WIS_County_D.svg *License*: Public Domain *Contributors*: Rocket000, SPUI

File:WIS County H.svg *Source*: http://bibliocm.bibliolabs.com/mwAnon/index.php?title=File:WIS_County_H.svg *License*: Public Domain *Contributors*: SPUI

File:WIS 73.svg *Source*: http://bibliocm.bibliolabs.com/mwAnon/index.php?title=File:WIS_73.svg *License*: Public Domain *Contributors*: Juliancolton, SPUI

File:WIS County M.svg *Source*: http://bibliocm.bibliolabs.com/mwAnon/index.php?title=File:WIS_County_M.svg *License*: Public Domain *Contributors*: SPUI

File:WIS County DD.svg *Source*: http://bibliocm.bibliolabs.com/mwAnon/index.php?title=File:WIS_County_DD.svg *License*: Public Domain *Contributors*: User:Master_son

File:WIS County E.svg *Source*: http://bibliocm.bibliolabs.com/mwAnon/index.php?title=File:WIS_County_E.svg *License*: Public Domain *Contributors*: SPUI

File:WIS County F.svg *Source*: http://bibliocm.bibliolabs.com/mwAnon/index.php?title=File:WIS_County_F.svg *License*: Public Domain *Contributors*: SPUI

File:WIS 97.svg *Source*: http://bibliocm.bibliolabs.com/mwAnon/index.php?title=File:WIS_97.svg *License*: Public Domain *Contributors*: Common Good, SPUI

File:WIS County S.svg *Source*: http://bibliocm.bibliolabs.com/mwAnon/index.php?title=File:WIS_County_S.svg *License*: Public Domain *Contributors*: SPUI

File:WIS 107.svg *Source*: http://bibliocm.bibliolabs.com/mwAnon/index.php?title=File:WIS_107.svg *License*: Public Domain *Contributors*: SPUI

File:WIS 52.svg *Source*: http://bibliocm.bibliolabs.com/mwAnon/index.php?title=File:WIS_52.svg *License*: Public Domain *Contributors*: Juliancolton, SPUI

File:WIS County NN.svg *Source*: http://bibliocm.bibliolabs.com/mwAnon/index.php?title=File:WIS_County_NN.svg *License*: Public Domain *Contributors*: User:Master_son

File:WIS County N.svg *Source*: http://bibliocm.bibliolabs.com/mwAnon/index.php?title=File:WIS_County_N.svg *License*: Public Domain *Contributors*: SPUI

File:I-39.svg *Source*: http://bibliocm.bibliolabs.com/mwAnon/index.php?title=File:I-39.svg *License*: unknown *Contributors*: Augiasstallputzer, Ltljltlj, SPUI, T2, Xnatedawgx, 1 anonymous edits

File:WIS County Q.svg *Source*: http://bibliocm.bibliolabs.com/mwAnon/index.php?title=File:WIS_County_Q.svg *License*: Public Domain *Contributors*: Rocket000, SPUI

File:WIS County Y.svg *Source*: http://bibliocm.bibliolabs.com/mwAnon/index.php?title=File:WIS_County_Y.svg *License*: Public Domain *Contributors*: SPUI

File:WIS 49.svg *Source*: http://bibliocm.bibliolabs.com/mwAnon/index.php?title=File:WIS_49.svg *License*: Public Domain *Contributors*: Juliancolton, SPUI

File:WIS County G.svg *Source*: http://bibliocm.bibliolabs.com/mwAnon/index.php?title=File:WIS_County_G.svg *License*: Public Domain *Contributors*: SPUI

File:WIS County U.svg *Source*: http://bibliocm.bibliolabs.com/mwAnon/index.php?title=File:WIS_County_U.svg *License*: Public Domain *Contributors*: SPUI

File:WIS County MMM.svg *Source*: http://bibliocm.bibliolabs.com/mwAnon/index.php?title=File:WIS_County_MMM.svg *License*: Public Domain *Contributors*: User:Master_son

File:WIS County CC.svg *Source*: http://bibliocm.bibliolabs.com/mwAnon/index.php?title=File:WIS_County_CC.svg *License*: Public Domain *Contributors*: User:Master_son

File:WIS 47.svg *Source*: http://bibliocm.bibliolabs.com/mwAnon/index.php?title=File:WIS_47.svg *License*: Public Domain *Contributors*: Juliancolton, SPUI

File:WIS 55.svg *Source*: http://bibliocm.bibliolabs.com/mwAnon/index.php?title=File:WIS_55.svg *License*: Public Domain *Contributors*: Juliancolton, SPUI

File:WIS County K.svg *Source*: http://bibliocm.bibliolabs.com/mwAnon/index.php?title=File:WIS_County_K.svg *License*: Public Domain *Contributors*: SPUI

File:WIS 117.svg *Source*: http://bibliocm.bibliolabs.com/mwAnon/index.php?title=File:WIS_117.svg *License*: Public Domain *Contributors*: Common Good, Juliancolton, SPUI

File:WIS County BE.svg *Source*: http://bibliocm.bibliolabs.com/mwAnon/index.php?title=File:WIS_County_BE.svg *License*: GNU Free Documentation License *Contributors*: User:Master_son

File:WIS 160.svg *Source*: http://bibliocm.bibliolabs.com/mwAnon/index.php?title=File:WIS_160.svg *License*: Public Domain *Contributors*: Juliancolton, SPUI

File:WIS 156.svg *Source*: http://bibliocm.bibliolabs.com/mwAnon/index.php?title=File:WIS_156.svg *License*: Public Domain *Contributors*: Common Good, Juliancolton, SPUI

File:WIS 32.svg *Source*: http://bibliocm.bibliolabs.com/mwAnon/index.php?title=File:WIS_32.svg *License*: Public Domain *Contributors*: Juliancolton, MrDolomite, SPUI

File:WIS County V.svg *Source*: http://bibliocm.bibliolabs.com/mwAnon/index.php?title=File:WIS_County_V.svg *License*: Public Domain *Contributors*: Rocket000, SPUI

File:WIS County C.svg *Source*: http://bibliocm.bibliolabs.com/mwAnon/index.php?title=File:WIS_County_C.svg *License*: Public Domain *Contributors*: SPUI

File:WIS County EB.svg *Source*: http://bibliocm.bibliolabs.com/mwAnon/index.php?title=File:WIS_County_EB.svg *License*: GNU Free Documentation License *Contributors*: User:Master_son

File:US 141 (WI).svg *Source*: http://bibliocm.bibliolabs.com/mwAnon/index.php?title=File:US_141_(WI).svg *License*: Public Domain *Contributors*: User:Master_son

File:WIS 54.svg *Source*: http://bibliocm.bibliolabs.com/mwAnon/index.php?title=File:WIS_54.svg *License*: Public Domain *Contributors*: Juliancolton, SPUI

File:WIS 57.svg *Source*: http://bibliocm.bibliolabs.com/mwAnon/index.php?title=File:WIS_57.svg *License*: Public Domain *Contributors*: Juliancolton, SPUI

File:WIS County P.svg *Source*: http://bibliocm.bibliolabs.com/mwAnon/index.php?title=File:WIS_County_P.svg *License*: Public Domain *Contributors*: SPUI

File:WIS County AB.svg *Source*: http://bibliocm.bibliolabs.com/mwAnon/index.php?title=File:WIS_County_AB.svg *License*: Public Domain *Contributors*: Fredddie

Image:WIS 23.svg *Source*: http://bibliocm.bibliolabs.com/mwAnon/index.php?title=File:WIS_23.svg *License*: Public Domain *Contributors*: Docu, Juliancolton, SPUI

Image Sources, Licenses and Contributors

Image:WIS 28.svg *Source*: http://bibliocm.bibliolabs.com/mwAnon/index.php?title=File:WIS_28.svg *License*: Public Domain *Contributors*: User:SPUI

Image:WIS County W.svg *Source*: http://bibliocm.bibliolabs.com/mwAnon/index.php?title=File:WIS_County_W.svg *License*: Public Domain *Contributors*: SPUI

File:I-43.svg *Source*: http://bibliocm.bibliolabs.com/mwAnon/index.php?title=File:I-43.svg *License*: unknown *Contributors*: Augiasstallputzer, Ltljltlj, Rocket000, SPUI

Image:WIS County XX.svg *Source*: http://bibliocm.bibliolabs.com/mwAnon/index.php?title=File:WIS_County_XX.svg *License*: Public Domain *Contributors*: User:Master_son

Image:US 151 (WI).svg *Source*: http://bibliocm.bibliolabs.com/mwAnon/index.php?title=File:US_151_(WI).svg *License*: Public Domain *Contributors*: User:Master_son

Image:US 10.svg *Source*: http://bibliocm.bibliolabs.com/mwAnon/index.php?title=File:US_10.svg *License*: Public Domain *Contributors*: Rocket000, SPUI

Image:WIS County F.svg *Source*: http://bibliocm.bibliolabs.com/mwAnon/index.php?title=File:WIS_County_F.svg *License*: Public Domain *Contributors*: SPUI

Image:MN-43.svg *Source*: http://bibliocm.bibliolabs.com/mwAnon/index.php?title=File:MN-43.svg *License*: Public Domain *Contributors*: User:Master_son

Image:US 53.svg *Source*: http://bibliocm.bibliolabs.com/mwAnon/index.php?title=File:US_53.svg *License*: Public Domain *Contributors*: Rocket000, SPUI

Image:WIS 93.svg *Source*: http://bibliocm.bibliolabs.com/mwAnon/index.php?title=File:WIS_93.svg *License*: Public Domain *Contributors*: Kanonkas, SPUI

Image:I-94.svg *Source*: http://bibliocm.bibliolabs.com/mwAnon/index.php?title=File:I-94.svg *License*: unknown *Contributors*: Augiasstallputzer, Ltljltlj, SPUI, 1 anonymous edits

Image:WIS 13.svg *Source*: http://bibliocm.bibliolabs.com/mwAnon/index.php?title=File:WIS_13.svg *License*: Public Domain *Contributors*: Juliancolton, SPUI

Image:WIS 73.svg *Source*: http://bibliocm.bibliolabs.com/mwAnon/index.php?title=File:WIS_73.svg *License*: Public Domain *Contributors*: Juliancolton, SPUI

Image:No image wide.svg *Source*: http://bibliocm.bibliolabs.com/mwAnon/index.php?title=File:No_image_wide.svg *License*: Public Domain *Contributors*: SPUI, TwinsMetsFan

Image:I-39.svg *Source*: http://bibliocm.bibliolabs.com/mwAnon/index.php?title=File:I-39.svg *License*: unknown *Contributors*: Augiasstallputzer, Ltljltlj, SPUI, T2, Xnatedawgx, 1 anonymous edits

Image:US 51.svg *Source*: http://bibliocm.bibliolabs.com/mwAnon/index.php?title=File:US_51.svg *License*: Public Domain *Contributors*: Bidgee, SPUI, 3 anonymous edits

Image:WIS 22.svg *Source*: http://bibliocm.bibliolabs.com/mwAnon/index.php?title=File:WIS_22.svg *License*: Public Domain *Contributors*: Juliancolton, SPUI

Image:WIS 49.svg *Source*: http://bibliocm.bibliolabs.com/mwAnon/index.php?title=File:WIS_49.svg *License*: Public Domain *Contributors*: Juliancolton, SPUI

Image:US 45.svg *Source*: http://bibliocm.bibliolabs.com/mwAnon/index.php?title=File:US_45.svg *License*: Public Domain *Contributors*: Luigi Chiesa, SPUI, Xnatedawgx

Image:WIS54EastTerminus.jpg *Source*: http://bibliocm.bibliolabs.com/mwAnon/index.php?title=File:WIS54EastTerminus.jpg *License*: Creative Commons Attribution-Sharealike 2.5 *Contributors*: Original uploader was Royalbroil at en.wikipedia

File:BuffaloCountyWisconsinWIS54WestTerminusBridge.jpg *Source*: http://bibliocm.bibliolabs.com/mwAnon/index.php?title=File:BuffaloCountyWisconsinWIS54WestTerminusBridge.jpg *License*: Creative Commons Attribution-Sharealike 3.0 *Contributors*: User:Royalbroil

Image:WIS 59.svg *Source*: http://bibliocm.bibliolabs.com/mwAnon/index.php?title=File:WIS_59.svg *License*: Public Domain *Contributors*: SPUI

File:WIS 56.svg *Source*: http://bibliocm.bibliolabs.com/mwAnon/index.php?title=File:WIS_56.svg *License*: Public Domain *Contributors*: SPUI

File:WIS 58.svg *Source*: http://bibliocm.bibliolabs.com/mwAnon/index.php?title=File:WIS_58.svg *License*: Public Domain *Contributors*: Juliancolton, SPUI

Image:SturgeonBayBridgeJuly2008WIS42WIS57.jpg *Source*: http://bibliocm.bibliolabs.com/mwAnon/index.php?title=File:SturgeonBayBridgeJuly2008WIS42WIS57.jpg *License*: Creative Commons Attribution-Sharealike 3.0 *Contributors*: User:Royalbroil

File:WIS 59.svg *Source*: http://bibliocm.bibliolabs.com/mwAnon/index.php?title=File:WIS_59.svg *License*: Public Domain *Contributors*: SPUI

File:US 18.svg *Source*: http://bibliocm.bibliolabs.com/mwAnon/index.php?title=File:US_18.svg *License*: Public Domain *Contributors*: SPUI, 1 anonymous edits

File:WIS 145.svg *Source*: http://bibliocm.bibliolabs.com/mwAnon/index.php?title=File:WIS_145.svg *License*: Public Domain *Contributors*: SPUI

File:WIS 190.svg *Source*: http://bibliocm.bibliolabs.com/mwAnon/index.php?title=File:WIS_190.svg *License*: Public Domain *Contributors*: SPUI

File:WIS 100.svg *Source*: http://bibliocm.bibliolabs.com/mwAnon/index.php?title=File:WIS_100.svg *License*: Public Domain *Contributors*: SPUI

File:WIS 167.svg *Source*: http://bibliocm.bibliolabs.com/mwAnon/index.php?title=File:WIS_167.svg *License*: Public Domain *Contributors*: Common Good, SPUI

File:WIS 60.svg *Source*: http://bibliocm.bibliolabs.com/mwAnon/index.php?title=File:WIS_60.svg *License*: Public Domain *Contributors*: Juliancolton, SPUI

File:WIS 33.svg *Source*: http://bibliocm.bibliolabs.com/mwAnon/index.php?title=File:WIS_33.svg *License*: Public Domain *Contributors*: Juliancolton, SPUI

File:WIS 84.svg *Source*: http://bibliocm.bibliolabs.com/mwAnon/index.php?title=File:WIS_84.svg *License*: Public Domain *Contributors*: Royalbroil, SPUI

File:WIS 144.svg *Source*: http://bibliocm.bibliolabs.com/mwAnon/index.php?title=File:WIS_144.svg *License*: Public Domain *Contributors*: Kanonkas, SPUI

File:WIS 23.svg *Source*: http://bibliocm.bibliolabs.com/mwAnon/index.php?title=File:WIS_23.svg *License*: Public Domain *Contributors*: Docu, Juliancolton, SPUI

File:WIS 67.svg *Source*: http://bibliocm.bibliolabs.com/mwAnon/index.php?title=File:WIS_67.svg *License*: Public Domain *Contributors*: Juliancolton, SPUI

File:WIS 149.svg *Source*: http://bibliocm.bibliolabs.com/mwAnon/index.php?title=File:WIS_149.svg *License*: Public Domain *Contributors*: Juliancolton, Luigi Chiesa, SPUI

File:US 151 (WI).svg *Source*: http://bibliocm.bibliolabs.com/mwAnon/index.php?title=File:US_151_(WI).svg *License*: Public Domain *Contributors*: User:Master_son

File:WIS 114.svg *Source*: http://bibliocm.bibliolabs.com/mwAnon/index.php?title=File:WIS_114.svg *License*: Public Domain *Contributors*: Common Good, Juliancolton, SPUI

File:WIS 96.svg *Source*: http://bibliocm.bibliolabs.com/mwAnon/index.php?title=File:WIS_96.svg *License*: Public Domain *Contributors*: Juliancolton, SPUI

File:WIS 172.svg *Source*: http://bibliocm.bibliolabs.com/mwAnon/index.php?title=File:WIS_172.svg *License*: Public Domain *Contributors*: Common Good, Juliancolton, SPUI

CPSIA information can be obtained at www.ICGtesting.com
Printed in the USA
LVOW11s1429150713

342853LV00020B/185/P